Through Eyes Like Mine

Noriko Nakada

"I am sitting here wanting
memories to teach me
to see the beauty in the world
through my own eyes."

~ Sweet Honey in the Rock

PART ONE

NAME

In the dark of early morning, frost turns the juniper trees silver in the moonlight. Dad drives down Franklin Avenue toward Hospital Hill. Spring awaits but the ground is still frozen. In the lingering winter cold Mom complains about her bare feet freezing inside her slippers. Bend's small town streets are dark and deserted so Mom asks Dad to run the light at Highway 97. He refuses. This is not their first baby. Dad knows there's no rush.

I resist entering the world, force Mom into back labor and at dawn my head pushes through. Too much pressure on my wide shoulders snaps my baby-soft collarbone like an old carrot.

The next day my parents carry me home to a house on Shepard Road. The front door swings open to brown shag carpet and lime-green and orange wallpaper. They place me in the warm, sticky hands of my six-year-old brother and four-year-old sister sitting side-by-side on the couch. My parents take pictures as Chet and Laura look down at me. My siblings think I'm the most beautiful baby in the world.

They name me Noriko Lisa Nakada. Mariko was their first choice but a cousin got to it first. My brother is named Chet Henry. He doesn't need a Japanese name. He's a boy and will keep Nakada when he marries. People will always know he's Japanese even though we're only half. My sister, Laura Yukiko, is named after the Japanese word for snow. Noriko is the name of a Japanese princess and Lisa is the name my sister picks. We both have a Japanese name for Dad and a regular name for Mom.

I am Noriko only to Dad. Mom calls me Riko for a while and then Nori. For some reason Chet calls me Rodriguez or Rod. Nori is the name that sticks. Nori, pronounced like Lori but with an N. Nori means seaweed, not princess.

DADDY

I wake up before the light. Cold, dry air hits my face and hands as I emerge from the warmth of bed. In the living room, Dad is just a shape in the dark. He crouches before the wood stove. Every morning, before the sun comes up and while everyone else sleeps, I help Dad start the fire.

My small hands crumple yesterday's slick newsprint. Dad places kindling and paper deep into the heart of the stove. When he strikes a match, the smell tickles my nose. Dad's steady hand lights the paper. The flames lick and spread. Soon the cold grows warm and the dark turns light. The wood pops and snaps. Dad pulls the heavy iron door, but leaves it open a crack, giving the fire room to breathe.

"Dad's home," Mom yells when she hears him pull up the driveway. I run to greet him and leap into his arms.

"*Yosho*," Dad grunts as he lifts me high above his head. Dad's strong even though he's older than other dads I know. His hair is the color of pepper and his face is tan from working in the garden in the summer, or skiing in the winter.

Later, Dad sits in the big lime-green armchair with the newspaper and I fold onto his lap. He reads and I tell him about my day. I pull the mechanical pencil out of his shirt pocket and click the long, thin thread of lead. I ask him what an engineer does all day, but never remember his answer.

We play Cat's Cradle with yellow yarn tied into a circle. Our hands and fingers dance in and out and around one another. We play Jon, Kim, Po where rock beats scissors, scissors beat paper, and paper beats rock.

I have an orange balloon from my second birthday party. I bat it around the living room. It floats, bounces and falls until it loses all its air and shrivels up.

SNOWFALL

I wrap my baby blanket tight around me and look out the sliding glass door into our backyard. Snowflakes drift down from the grey sky and smoke floats up from brick chimneys. The world has turned white and perfect. The dead, brown grass and rough rooftops hide beneath a fresh, smooth blanket. Standing close to the door, the cold creeps in. My breath fogs up the glass and I wipe it clean in order to watch my brother and sister making first steps in the snow.

Laura walks carefully toward the middle of the backyard as if she doesn't want to mess it up and then falls back into the fresh powder. She waves her arms and legs leaving the imprint of an angel. Chet is different. He runs through the cold kicking up a sparkling cloud of white behind him. Laura stands up just as Chet tosses a snowball in her direction. Soon they are running, jumping, and throwing. Their breath puffs out in front of them, misty clouds that disappear and reappear, disappear and reappear.

I wish I was out there with them, but I'm sick. My face is hot and my back is sweaty. A gust of wind sends clumps of snow falling from the trees. Goosebumps rise on my skin and suddenly instead of feeling hot, I'm cold. I pull my blanket tighter around my shoulders and wish Chet and Laura would come inside. The smell of snow would come in with them and they would strip off their hats, jackets, and mittens. Mom would make hot chocolate and all of us would sit at the kitchen table, sipping cocoa and warming our hands on the cups.

A SMALL WORLD

I stand in the kitchen holding a green, plastic Tupperware cup. Chet and Craigor tell me to drink it. Laura watches from the hallway. She says nothing but makes a face at Chet and Craigor. Maybe this look means she wants them to stop or maybe she's just tired of their teasing. I look into the cup, unsure of what to do.

"It's lemonade," Chet says. "It tastes really good."

The liquid in the cup is yellow like lemons but it doesn't smell like lemons. I don't know why they are all watching me.

Laura stands there, glaring at the boys. Usually if Laura is mad she just tells Chet to stop, but ever since Craigor came, things have changed.

Craigor is our cousin from Los Angeles. He's been living with us all summer. He has hair that's curly and almost red. His eyes are green and he's older and taller than Chet. If you look at him with his white skin and freckles and then look at us, brown from the summer sun, it's hard to believe we're related at all.

Sometimes Craigor is mean. He bosses Chet and Laura around and pushes when he gets mad. But if Chet or Laura argue back, he's the one who starts crying and then says he's sorry. He doesn't do anything bad to me though. He says I'm the cutest baby in the world.

Craigor gets a look in his eye, and sometimes Chet does too, like they are up to no good. But most of the time Craigor's eyes are sad, even when he smiles. At night, when the house is quiet, I hear him crying.

No one tells me why Craigor is living with us, but I think something is wrong with his parents. One day, Mom talks on the phone with one of her sisters. I watch the long, yellow phone cord twist around Mom's ankles. She says, "He can stay with us until she gets it together." Mom never says anything about Craigor's dad.

I examine the liquid in the green cup again. I've been holding the plastic for so long, it's warm in my hand. I raise the cup to my lips and out of the corner of my eye I see Chet and Craigor smiling at one another. I tilt the cup back but Laura snatches it from my hand.

"No," the boys yell, as Laura runs with the cup to the kitchen sink.

"Mom," Laura yells as she pours the cup out. "Craigor and Chet are making Nori drink their pee."

The boys laugh. "She never drank it. We wouldn't have let her do it," Chet says, but I don't believe him.

I run my hand along the rough orange and green striped wallpaper in the hallway and shut my bedroom door tight behind me.

All summer long Chet and Craigor catch bugs and frogs outside and torture them. They make mud and throw it all over the yard. Laura, who used to play with Chet, plays inside with me now. She shows me how to hold a pencil and teaches me how to write my name.

When winter comes the boys have to be inside. Instead of killing bugs or small animals, they pick on Laura. Laura is strong though, and she takes it. She even breaks her leg trying to keep up with them on the ski slopes. She has to lay on the couch in the living room with her leg in a cast while Craigor and Chet tease her. The hard, chalky cast runs all the way from her toes to her waist. She looks miserable and bored on the couch. She says her leg itches underneath that white crust.

Laura doesn't like to be alone with Craigor. She sends me to get Mom when he bothers her. Sometimes Mom comes, but when she's too busy, I feel like I've let my sister down. I run outside, even though it's cold, and hide between the rows of dead corn in Dad's garden.

One reflector, two reflector, three reflector, four... the world speeds by in a blur as we wind over this mountain road. On car trips I stare out the window and count reflectors as they flash by in the night. One reflector, two reflector, three reflector... When I'm not counting, I sing, or recite nursery rhymes, "The three little kittens, they lost their mittens, and they began to cry..."

We're driving from Oregon to California to drop Craigor off with his Mom. Then we're going to Disneyland. Mom points to the sign that says we're leaving Oregon and I enter California for the first time.

I sit up front, between Mom and Dad on the long bench seat of the station wagon. The muscles in Dad's arms flex as he steers and shifts gears. I watch Mom's hands as she files her nails. Her wedding ring glints in what's left of the sunlight. Mom's ring isn't like any ring I've ever seen. It's big and shaped like a heavy teardrop that doesn't want to fall. When Mom's done filing her nails, she hands me her ring. She reaches for a little yellow bottle of lotion she keeps in the dashboard. I hold the ring in my fingers and breathe in the smell of moisturizer while Mom rubs her hands together. As the sun goes down, I watch the day's last light dance off Mom's diamond.

The headlights make a white triangle of light on the highway and I start counting again. One reflector, two reflector, three... Chet and Craigor sleep in the back seat. Laura lies in the back of the station wagon with her broken leg propped up on pillows.

Disneyland is the happiest place on earth for a little girl with a broken leg. Mickey, Minnie, Donald, and Goofy all come over to talk to my big sister. They put their hands over their mouths, shocked to see a little girl in a wheelchair with a broken leg. Minnie pretends to cry. Goofy spins Laura around in the chair and Mickey signs her cast. We take a picture in front of Sleeping Beauty's castle with all of the Disney characters.

Craigor isn't with us any more. We left him at a house with curtains drawn tight and air heavy with cigarette smoke. His mom was so happy to see him. She hugged him until they both cried.

I kind of wish Craigor had been able to come with us because Disneyland is the happiest place on earth. Maybe if he had, he wouldn't feel so sad.

Laura is back to playing with Chet. They go on the big kid rides: the Teacups and Matterhorn. Dad goes with them and Mom stays with me. I want to ride Small World again. We wait in front of a huge, glittering clock. The gears spin and hands swing, tick tock, tick tock. We make it to the front of the line and Mom lifts me into the boat. We float into a bright world of kids and I sing along as we float from Africa to Europe, Australia to Japan.

"It's a world of laughter a world of tears."

I study the clothes and hair of these kids from far away places.

"It's a world of hopes and a world of fears."

I search the faces as they spin and dance, looking for Laura, or Chet, or Craigor.

"There's so much that we share..."

A girl with a broken leg, a boy with a smirk or sad eyes.

"Now it's time we're aware..."

Somewhere, singing and bobbing up and down, I search for a girl like me.

"It's a small world after all."

CHRISTMAS 1976

I lean against a cupboard in the kitchen on Christmas Day and watch strangers fill our house. Dad's brothers and sisters are in town, all my uncles and aunties and their kids. There are too many for me to count. In every corner two or three uncles sit talking, playing cards, sipping short glasses filled with ice and rum. The boy cousins are mean. They ignore me and run all over the house. My girl cousins are tall and thin. They sit quietly and push long, thick, black hair behind their ears. I'm the littlest of all the cousins and I don't say much. At the kitchen table, my cousins Pat and Mari show Laura and me how to fold origami. My fingers can't make the clean, straight creases in the colored paper. Laura folds bright green paper into a frog that jumps. Pat makes a white crane and Mari folds a blue box. Mochi, our little dog, sleeps under the table, trying to escape all of these people.

Auntie Grace stirs gravy in the kitchen while Auntie Hannah, Auntie Jo, and Auntie Virginia lift lids off steaming pots, tasting and measuring. I try to remember which kids belong to which Aunties but the names get mixed up in my head.

They're in Mom's kitchen, but Mom just watches or points to where we keep the salt. Auntie Grace is the one who tells everyone what to do. Mom stands out among all my Japanese aunties with her auburn hair and loud voice. She is at least three inches taller than each of them and she's the only white person in the house. No one sees this, though, or maybe I'm the only one who notices how different my mom is from everyone else. But we're different too, my brother, my sister, and me. It's easy to tell that we belong to our mom. We're the ones with hair that's brown instead of black, the ones with wide brown eyes instead of dark Asian ones. No one talks about it, but everyone knows Chet, Laura and I are different.

Earlier this morning, when it was just our family of five, Chet woke everyone up. It was still dark out and Dad started a fire in the woodstove. We opened our presents in a flurry of ripping paper and easy grins. Santa brought me a whole box full of rings, a doll I can take in the bath, and a Kermit the Frog puppet. We got all dressed up for church. Laura and I wore matching dresses, Chet a suit, and we posed for a picture in front of the tree.

At church, two altar boys carried little baby Jesus to the manger at the front of the church. Another boy swung a long, metal chain with incense pouring out. We sat in the front row so I could look at the nativity scene. When it was time for Communion, Father James placed his dry hands on the top of my head for a blessing because I haven't had my First Communion yet. The church was crowded because lots of families come for mass only on Easter and Christmas and not every single Sunday like we do. I knelt and watched the families file through for Communion: the Butlers, the Kukars, the Duncans, the Corrigans and the Hurleys all dressed up for Christmas. I realized Mom looked a lot like the rest of the church. Her auburn hair blended right in while Dad, Chet, Laura and I stood out with darker hair than everyone else. I wondered what the other families in Bend did for Christmas. What did they eat? What did their aunts, uncles, and cousins look like?

That church world feels far away from the scene of aunties, uncles and cousins filling our house with rice and tea alongside turkey, stuffing and mashed potatoes. Mom sets the table and this family of strangers spread throughout the house to eat dinner off paper plates. Uncles and Aunties sit in the dining room or at card tables set up in the living room. Cousins perch on couches or sit on the floor balancing plates on their knees.

One of my uncles from LA, Uncle Yoshinao, brought a piñata. After dinner, he hangs the red paper-maiche reindeer in the family room. We take turns hitting it with Chet's baseball bat. Even without the blindfold, I can't break it open, but when it's Chet's turn he swings wildly and candy streams out. We rush in after the peppermints and caramels mixed in with crepe paper. I unwrap a candy strawberry and wonder if anyone else in Bend had a piñata on Christmas.

In the morning all of my uncles, aunties and cousins leave. They drive away from our little town back to California or Alaska or Maryland. Our family, which seems so different from all of the other families in Bend, settles in for the long Central Oregon winter.

PAIN

The afternoon is quiet with Chet and Laura at school. Mom's radio is on low in the kitchen. In the dining room, my toddler knees dig into the cold laminate. The texture makes indentations in my soft skin, leaving lines like a quilt on my knees. I twist the metal butterfly knob on Carrie, my little blonde-haired walking doll. I want her little rubber soles to walk across the floor, but Mochi's tail keeps knocking her down. I yell, "No, Mochi," but he never listens to me unless I pull his tail. He yips and scampers off.

Now Carrie and I can play alone. I balance her carefully, and let go of the butterfly knob. The knob whines and spins and Carrie teeters across the floor until she smacks into a table leg. From the corner of my eye, I spot Mochi scurrying back into the kitchen. He snatches Carrie between his tiny jaws and runs away.

I find Carrie a few days later, buried in the backyard, her blonde hair matted and dirty and the left side of her face punctured by teeth marks.

Mochi and I play in the family room beneath the wobbly card table. He snaps at me; I squeal. I tug his tail; he lunges. I pull back and hit my head. Mochi's small, white teeth connect with the left side of my face. Blood streams from above my eye. Mom and Dad come in and take Mochi away.

I get a butterfly band-aid.

Later I ask Mom, "Where's Mochi?"

"He's gone."

I never see Mochi again.

I peer out the back window of our Plymouth station wagon into the parking lot of the swimming pool. Mom parked the car in the shade of a big pine tree, but I'm still hot, sweaty and itchy from the chicken pox.

Chet and Laura are in a swim meet. Mom will stop by to check on me between races. I picture being at the pool instead of in the car. With my eyes closed, I can smell the chlorine. I've been to so many meets it's easy for me to picture Laura getting ready for the 50 free. She shakes her legs and when the man with the bullhorn says, "Take your mark," she climbs up on her block. Laura leans over on "set," and when the starter fires a cap gun all the swimmers dive into the smooth water. They come up swimming fast, making the water boil and churn.

I open my eyes. I'm still in the car with pink lotion on the bumps. Mom says not to scratch or I'll leave scars. I imagine cool water on my feet, but if I go in the pool I'll give everyone chicken pox. I'm contagious so I have to spend the whole day in the car, bored, sweating and trying not to scratch.

Kindergarten is still two years away, so after we drop Laura and Chet off at school, Mom and I go grocery shopping at Safeway.

We pass by the flower department and enter the fruit and vegetable section. I'm walking too slowly so Mom puts me in the cart. She picks through a pile of apples. It's quiet in the grocery store this early in the morning. A man sprays the lettuce with a little hose. "Hi there, Mrs. Nakada."

Mom smiles and hands me a brown paper bag of shiny red apples. We walk toward the cereal aisle and she picks out Corn Flakes and Cheerios, never Coco Puffs or Cap'n Crunch. I remember that I have my little music box in my jacket pocket. It is brown and shaped like a drumstick. I hold the handle with one hand and turn the little red knob with the other. The box sings, "To dream, the impossible dream," and Mom hums along but she doesn't quite hit the right notes. The front of the music box is clear so I can see the tiny metal parts turning inside.

"Where did you get that darling girl?" Asks a woman with hair so white it's almost purple. She pats the top of my head.

"Oh, she's mine," Mom says and she cuts the words short as if she doesn't want to talk about where I came from.

"Oh," the woman replies and she shuffles toward the frozen food section.

Mom isn't humming anymore. She's done and we head toward the cash register. Mom sighs, writes a check for the groceries, and then loads the bags and me into the back of the car. I guard the grocery bags on the drive home. If I don't, they might fall over. I watch the bags and hum "Impossible Dream" because I can't play with my music box and guard the bags at the same time.

We get home and Mom opens the back of the car. I pull out my music box again. Mom grabs the bags and tells me to jump. I do, but the ground sneaks up on me. I fall, and try to catch myself but the music box knob pokes into my face. There's blood on the ground, on my hand, and Mom drops the groceries. The bags fall over and red apples roll across the driveway.

Mom tells me to hold something against my face while we drive to the doctor. My pediatrician, Dr. Brown, says I need stitches. She gets a needle and thread just like Mom does when there's a hole in one of Dad's socks. Dr. Brown asks me if I'm ready. I nod and hold Mom's hand. Mom tells me to squeeze if it hurts. Dr. Brown wipes my cheek and the skin stings from the cold. Then I watch her hand. At first it looks like that tiny needle is coming right at my eye. I watch the black thread come and go, come and go. After a few stitches Dr. Brown turns to Mom and says, "I forgot to tell her to close her eyes." She turns back to me. "You can close your eyes if you want, Nori." I can't close my eyes now, though. I watch Dr. Brown work until she's done.

CHESS

Laura and Chet are playing chess. Laura studies the board and then turns to watch the TV as if she doesn't care where any of those white and black pieces are. But I know she's just pretending not to care. It's Chet's move and he's losing. Laura is black and she has Chet's queen, bishops, a tower and three pawns. I wonder how many moves she is from winning.

Chet hates to lose. He's older and a boy so he thinks he should win at everything. Chet edges a pawn forward and takes one of Laura's towers. He smiles until Laura looks back at the board and grins. I don't see what she sees on the red and black chessboard, but Chet must because he flings the board onto the floor and tells Laura, "Oh well, I guess we'll never know who won."

Laura's eyes fill with tears. She glares at the chess pieces scattered on the carpet. Chet storms out of the family room and into the kitchen but we all know who won.

BIG BROTHER

God talks to Mom. He tells her things when she prays. I wonder if I pray long or hard enough he'll talk to me, but he hasn't yet. We go to church every Sunday, no matter what. Afterwards, we come straight home. We never go out for breakfast or stop for doughnuts. Maybe God talks to Mom because it takes a lot of faith to get all of us up for church by 8:30 every Sunday. Maybe it's because Mom never gives into temptations like restaurant hash browns or maple bars even when all three of us whine from the back seat of the car.

After church, we sit around the kitchen table eating an early dinner like we always do on Sundays. I study the flower pattern in the wallpaper and play with my green beans. They're cold and hard. If I stall long enough maybe Mom won't make me eat them.

"Remember when we talked to you a while ago about getting a new brother?" Mom fills my cup with milk.

Laura and Chet stop playing with their green beans and stare at Mom. A few months ago we met this baby another family adopted. That little baby cried and cried until Mom picked her up. Mom said it was a sign from God that our family should adopt a baby too.

"Well, we got a picture in the mail yesterday."

She shows us a photo of a boy and tells us he will be our new brother. He's standing on a wooden swing, clinging to a rope. He's looking right into the camera, but the person taking the picture forgot to tell him to smile.

"His name is Aum Young Tak."

He's the same color grey as the dirt covering the playground. One look at the picture and I know I don't want him. He looks sad. He's already bigger than me, and older. I don't want a six-year-old brother. I want someone else to be the littlest, a baby, fresh and new. I look at this boy with a dirty face and empty eyes. I think he might not have a very good life if he stays in Korea. He will get a big tummy like the kids I see in Maryknoll Magazine. They aren't fat though. They're starving.

"We pick him up next month."

Next month. I wonder how many days that will be. I look down at my plate. He's coming whether I want him to or not. He will be my new big brother. I force the green beans in my mouth and swallow them like pills with the rest of my milk.

I count down to the day we will get a new brother, and on day 12, after Dad gets home from work, we go downtown to the police station to get fingerprinted. The station is filled with light so bright it makes my skin look green. We wait behind a counter while one of the policemen takes out a big book and a black inkpad. Dad goes first, then Mom, Chet and Laura. When it's my turn I have to stand on a stool so I can reach the pad of ink. The policeman takes my left hand first and starts with my pinkie. His hands are warm and he rolls each finger in the ink and then on the paper. I watch and wonder what getting a new brother has to do with my fingertips.

On the three-hour drive to the airport to pick up our new brother, it rains. Water pelts the windshield as we drive over the Cascade pass. The car is quiet except for the rhythm of the wiper blades smearing water from side to side. We arrive at the airport and walk down a long, blue hallway. It leads us to a room filled with windows. Chet, Laura and I press up against the glass leaving long smears with our chins and hands. We peer outside through the rain at the airplane, the biggest thing we've ever seen.

A hatch opens in the side of the plane and people step off into the wind and rain. Women look down over the babies in their arms, watching each step, shielding their cargo from the cold. Couples like Mom and Dad receive warm blanket bundles with tears in their eyes. I watch the door carefully and try to remember the photo. I don't see anyone who looks like my new brother yet.

"Maybe he changed his mind." I tell Mom, pulling the bottom of her coat. "Maybe he didn't want to come."

A woman walks toward us carrying a boy. The boy is bigger than me. He kicks and screams words I can't understand.

He doesn't want to go with us, but Dad picks him up anyway. He carries him like a sack of potatoes all the way through the airport. I have to run to keep up.

"Let him go back, Dad," I yell, but Dad doesn't say anything and his face twists like I've never seen before. The boy screams louder even though Dad is telling him it's okay. My face turns hot as I run after Dad and I wish that boy didn't have to come home with us.

My new brother sits in the front seat between Mom and Dad where I used to sit. I can smell him in the front seat. It's not a bad smell, just different, unfamiliar, like he's come from somewhere very far away. I feel sorry for him, being taken away by strangers to a place he's never been. I could tell him everything will be okay, but I don't know if it will, and he couldn't understand me anyway.

"Why's he so sad?"

Mom tells me something about Dad's grey hair and how he probably doesn't want an old dad. I don't think of Dad as old. The tears dry on my cheeks by the time we leave the airport but my new brother's cries fade to whimpers and his whimpers don't stop the whole drive home.

Mom and Dad give our new brother a new name even though he already had one. Mitch Aum Nakada. They don't talk about the name with us. He still has a Korean middle name. Would people in Korea mind a Korean boy suddenly having a Japanese last name?

That night our new brother doesn't want to sleep in the bunk beds in Chet's room, so we bring blankets and pillows into the living room. Chet holds his pillow that smells like drool and when Laura lays her blanket down he smacks her. Laura and I grab our pillows, and chase after Chet, taking turns getting him back. Mitch watches until we take a break. We sit on the floor, Chet, Laura and I, catching our breath, and that's when Mitch reveals his first smile. I think maybe he'll be okay. We wrap up in blankets and fall asleep together on the living room floor.

Four days later it's Halloween. Mom and Dad seem to have forgotten all about it so I have to be an angel for the second year in a row. Chet is a pirate with a sword and Laura is the Easter bunny. Mom doesn't think Mitch should dress up and go trick-or-treating but we convince her that it would be mean to leave him at home while we collect candy. Mom ends up putting Mitch in Laura's pink clown costume from a couple years ago. Mitch doesn't know that boys in America don't wear pink. We head out into the night and Mitch collects just as much candy as they rest of us even though he can't say trick-or-treat.

Dad brings home some kim chee when he makes a trip to Portland and I'm scared to taste it. It smells like something died in that glass jar. Dad eats some and his face starts to sweat, but Mitch finishes half the jar, no problem.

A reporter from *The Bend Bulletin* comes to our house to talk about the new addition to our family. He asks Mom and Dad questions and I watch him scribble notes on a little pad of paper. A couple days later there is a picture and story in the paper and Mitch makes our family famous. I climb onto a chair at the kitchen table, fold my knees beneath me, and gaze into the picture. We're all sitting on the couch in front of the window with the drapes drawn. I'm on Mom's lap and Mitch is on Dad's. Laura and Chet squeeze in so we all fit on the flowered couch. Everyone's smiling except me. I move my face closer and closer to the picture until all I see are little tiny dots.

Mom orders dinner from Eagle's Nest Pizza. It's our favorite, but Mitch won't eat it. "No wonder he's so skinny," I say. Laura gives me a dirty look, but I don't know why. He can't understand anything we say. He only speaks Korean. Dad cooks up a batch of *okazu*—stir-fried vegetables—and serves it with rice. Mitch doesn't touch his pizza, but he eats Dad's *okazu* with chopsticks.

Mitch gets to start kindergarten even though he doesn't speak any English yet. I'm used to seeing Chet and Laura walk away from me, but it's strange seeing Mitch starting an adventure all by himself. I wonder if he'll be all right in that room by himself where nobody knows that he isn't like the rest of us, that he's different.

When Mitch first came, neighbors sent casseroles and people stared as we walked to our regular pew at the front of the church. Now, the casseroles are gone and the newspaper clipping on the fridge has turned yellow. No one stares at us even though our family is even more different now than we were before. Mitch starts to eat hamburgers and French fries. He wears tennis shoes, Chet's hand-me down t-shirts and old blue jeans. He sleeps on the top bunk. Dad shows him how to ride a bike. He forgets how to use chopsticks. He goes silent. He stops trying to explain things in words I can't understand. Instead, he listens. He watches *Sesame Street* and *The Electric Company* with me but never sings, "Can you tell me how to get, how to get to Sesame Street?" Then, one night after *Mork and Mindy*, Mitch breaks his silence. "Nanu, nanu." He holds his hand up and moves his fingers just like Mork.

Mom takes the little rubber shoes and the red sweat suit Mitch wore the day he came from Korea and wraps them in tissue. She pulls the faded newspaper article off the fridge and smoothes the wrinkled paper. She opens her desk drawer and takes out the photo we received months ago. She places all these things in a shoebox and puts it in the closet where it will be safe until Mitch opens it someday like a present.

SPANKING

"You're so spoiled," Chet tells me. "Dad's never given you a bare-bottom spanking."

"Lucky you," says Laura. "He makes you reach down and grab your ankles."

I feel bad for Chet and Laura but I also feel left out. They have something together, from before I was born, something I can't touch.

I can't believe Dad would do something like that. Not Dad who lets me curl up on his lap and takes me out for ice cream. Dad would never hit me like that. He spanked me once on the bottom as I stood up from the table. It was more of a stinging tap like when a book is slammed shut. Even though it didn't really hurt, I cried. I was confused and knew I should try my best not to spill my milk again.

Mitch gets a bare-bottom spanking a few weeks after he comes. I don't know why, and I sit on my bed with the door closed. I stare at the wood grain in the door and wonder why I'm the only one who doesn't get bare-bottom spankings. Now, Chet, Laura and Mitch all have something together that I don't. Maybe it's because I'm the youngest, and even though Mitch came after me, I'm still littler. I know Chet and Laura will say I'm spoiled and get whatever I want. I don't care, though. I just hope I never do anything so bad that Dad gives me a bare-bottom spanking.

APPENDICITIS

Dad and Laura go for a run as the sun begins to set. Dad usually runs in the morning before work, but Laura has the Hershey track meet coming up and Dad is helping her train. They head up the hill on Shepard Road to the track at Pilot Butte. I lean over the back of the couch and look out the picture window at Laura's long, lean strides and Dad's short choppy ones carrying them up the road until they disappear into the orange light. I stare out the window at the growing darkness, waiting for them to come back.

Mom calls me to the kitchen. "I wonder where your father and Laura are." She hands me the plates for the table. "They should be back by now."

I set out the plates, knives and forks and then return to the couch. I cup my hands around my eyes and press up against the window. The whole world beyond our porch is swallowed by darkness. Mom tells me to wash my hands for dinner. Over the sound of running water in the bathroom, I hear the door open and close. Dad and Laura are back. I dry my hands on my pants and run out to greet them.

They're both out of breath and Dad looks pale. He doesn't smile. "Your sister sure is getting fast."

I wonder what's wrong when Dad goes into the bedroom and we eat dinner without him.

I hear footsteps and muffled voices in the night. Light from the hallway filters beneath my bedroom door. The front door opens and shuts and the car starts in the driveway. Before I can wonder where it's going, I drift back to sleep.

The next day we go to the hospital. Dad is there because of appendicitis. It has to do with something in your stomach that you don't need and if it explodes that's bad, but Dad's didn't explode. They took his appendix out and he has to stay in the hospital one more night. When we pull into the parking lot at the St. Charles Medical Center, Mitch doesn't want to go in. He starts to cry and Mom has to pick him up and carry him like a baby even though he's bigger than I am. I've gotten used to this. Mitch has only been here a few weeks and the last time we brought him to the hospital the doctor had to do something to his boy parts. Mitch screamed and cried. He probably thinks it will be like that when we visit Dad, but he settles down when we get to Dad's room on the third floor that smells like medicine and old people.

Dad lets me play with the switch that moves the bed up and down. He doesn't look pale and sick like he did last night, but he looks small in that big bed.

When Dad comes home the next day Mom makes his favorite meal, stuffed bell peppers. She makes Dad promise never to run with Laura again.

ON SKIS

Snow falls outside the car windows like stars glowing against a darkening night. White banks grow tall around us as Dad guides the car down a blank road. Mom hates driving in the snow. She reads a book and holds her breath every time Dad hits the brakes to test the slickness of the road.

We're almost to Tahoe where we'll spend Christmas with Dad's family. I've never spent Christmas away from Bend, but this year there are lots of changes. This year we have Mitch and this year I get to ski with the rest of the family. Even though I have lots of changes, Mitch has even more. Mitch has never seen snow before or celebrated Christmas. They don't even have Jesus in Korea.

Up on the mountain I've never seen so much snow. The white sky blurs and swirls around us covering the rooftops and cars, trees and roads. I've never been so cold. The wind snaps at my face and blows my hat away. Dad says if I'm big enough to ski I'm big enough to carry my own equipment. I chase down my hat and struggle from the car carrying my poles, skis, gloves, goggles, and hat. I trudge toward the mountain in heavy boots that pull me to the ground with every slick step.

Mitch gets into his bindings on his own so I have to too. Chet and Laura ski off with our cousins while Mitch and I push awkwardly on our poles. We follow Mom and Dad to the lift line.

The chair lift is all about timing. Dad tells us to watch for a few minutes until we recognize the pattern. "Follow the chair in front of you, move fast, look over your shoulder and then, up you go into the air."

We slide into line, Dad with me and Mom with Mitch and when it's my turn I follow all of the steps but that chair comes so fast and I'm so little that Dad has to lift me up so my bottom reaches. The chair sways and I'm flying, wind in my face, high above the slope, up in the trees with the clouds and snow.

Getting off the chair isn't any easier. Signs on the side of the lift instruct me to prepare to unload and keep my tips up. Once we get to the top I stand exactly when Dad says to and glide off the lift. Going is easy. It's stopping that's hard.

By the day after Christmas Mitch and I can both get on and off the lift, no problem. We follow Dad or Mom down the mountain in a long trail of turns, and on the long drive home, I dream of life above the bunny slope.

UNDERWATER

Spring means dressing up for Easter. It means the snow melts, the ground thaws, and my birthday is coming. But this spring, Mitch's first spring, it feels like our house sinks underwater.

It is April, and Chet and Laura are home for spring break. Chet and a friend from his fifth grade class ride their bikes all over town. At the crosswalk at Highway 97 and Revere, by the Wagner's grocery store, Chet and Greg Bob wait for the light. They hit the walk button and hold onto the pole, balancing on their bikes. When the walk sign flashes, Chet lets Greg Bob go first. Chet pushes off the sidewalk right as a truck swipes through the intersection and hits his friend.

Greg Bob was wearing red tennis shoes. Laura and Chet each have a pair of those same shoes. They were on sale at Payless. Greg Bob's shoes come off when the truck hits him, and when Mom picks up Chet, she gathers those red tennis shoes and returns them to Greg Bob's mother.

No one tells me what is happening. Mom has to go to the hospital and she tells Laura, Mitch and me to pray for Greg Bob, but I forget.

Later that afternoon, when Mom and Chet come home, they don't say anything. The second they open the door all the air is sucked out of the house and I know, prayers or no prayers, Greg Bob is gone. Chet doesn't say anything. He doesn't look at us. He doesn't seem to see us at all. He looks so far away even though he's standing right in front of me. He walks down the hallway and into his bedroom, closing the door behind him.

The world turns quiet, like I'm underwater. When you're underwater everything and everyone moves in slow motion. You have to hold your breath as long as you can before coming up for air.

At dinner that night I wait for someone, anyone—Mom, Dad, Chet, Laura, or Mitch—to break the silence, to push up through the surface for air, but no one talks. All I hear are forks scraping on heavy, green plates. Every second feels like forever. The hands on the clock move but our whole family, the whole house, sits underwater.

We dress up like we're going to church but it's a Monday night. We load into the station wagon and sit in the same heavy silence we've been swimming through for days. Mom and Dad discussed whether or not to take Mitch and me but they couldn't find a sitter so here we are, driving at dusk toward the mortuary on the other side of Pilot Butte. Even though it's spring, it still looks and feels like winter. The trees are bare, their thin, naked arms black against the grey and pink sky. The only sound—other than the six of us breathing—is the crack and snap of cinders hitting the underside of the car.

Inside the mortuary, dim light soaks into the wine-red carpet and rows of dark wooden benches. Our family fills up the second bench and we wait. I still feel like I'm underwater and hold my breath. Greg Bob's family enters from a special door and sits behind a curtain of beads. They aren't crying and they move in slow motion. People behind me sniff and sigh but I don't cry. A casket rests at the front of the room next to huge flowers. Greg Bob's body is in there, but it could have been Chet and then we would be sitting behind that beaded curtain.

Mom hands me a rosary of wooden beads and we begin to pray. We start with The Apostles Creed, and then fall into a rhythm of ten Hail Maries and an Our Father. I study the beads and move my fingers from one bead to the next to keep track of the beginning and end of each prayer. I watch the rosary beads instead of looking at Greg Bob's casket or his family.

We say one final prayer, one I don't know the words to, and then we are done. I wait for everyone to leave the mortuary, but instead each row stands to walk by Greg Bob's casket. Mom says I don't have to look in the casket and I don't know if I want to see Greg Bob after a car hit him. I want to say goodbye, though, so I follow Laura. We walk so fast that I only glance inside, but that boy, the boy lying inside, doesn't look like Greg Bob. He looks like a boy who is pale and sick and all dressed up so he can't go outside and play. I feel so sad I think I might cry because Greg Bob can never go outside and play again. I hold back my tears and walk to the dark parking lot. I stand at the car and wait for the rest of my family.

Greg Bob's mom gives Laura piano lessons and shortly after Greg Bob dies, there's a recital. Mom thought it would be cancelled but it isn't. We're still underwater. It is quiet and heavy and hard to breathe at our house but it's even worse in the car. On the way to the recital we have to drive through the intersection where Greg Bob died. Laura sits in the front seat and I'm in the back with Chet on my left and Mitch on my right. I hate sitting in the middle but the weight of the silence tells me not to complain. Mom drives slowly and when the light turns green the whole car slows down and Mom looks at Chet in the rear-view mirror. Chet looks toward the mountains in the west as we pass the spot where Greg Bob died.

At the recital, in Greg Bob's mom's living room, Laura plays a song. She hasn't practiced since Greg Bob died and she's still underwater. I listen and watch her fingers. She starts off all right but then the notes get all mixed up. Laura's face turns red and she looks like she might cry. She stands up and pushes the piano bench back. She doesn't bow or smile like the other kids did.

On the way home, before we pass through the intersection again, we wait for the light to turn, the same light where the man didn't wait. He drove right through and hit Greg Bob. Chet watched him get whisked away and now he's gone but Chet is still here. Mom looks at Chet in the passenger seat but he turns around to the back seat and gives Laura a wicked smile, a smile we haven't seen in over a week. "Dunt. Dunt. Dunt." He sings. "Another one bites the dust."

Mitch is the first to laugh and that's when we all come up for air and breathe again.

THE KING AND I

Mom drives us to a building by the Wendy's on the south side of town. The room is empty except for some folding chairs and lines of people. Voices echo off the high ceiling. A bunch of kids stand against a wall.

"Well, you're the only ones," Mom says as she leads us to the back of the line. She thought maybe some other Asian kids would show up to audition for *The King and I*. This confirms what we suspected—we are the only ones in the entire town. No other Japanese or Chinese kids and Mitch is the only Korean. There are no Black kids or Spanish kids like on *Sesame Street*. Bend isn't *Sesame Street*.

We stand in line and wait for the skinny woman holding a Polaroid camera to take our picture. We watch the kids in front of us sing the Happy Birthday song even though it's no one's birthday. When it's our turn, Chet goes first, then Laura and then me. Mitch gets to watch because he doesn't know the Happy Birthday song yet. I think Mom should have him try because Mitch is the only one who's 100% Asian instead of half, like us. He has no idea what's going on though, so it's my turn. My voice shakes and then disappears into the noise of the room.

The next day Mom answers the phone and with a smile she tells us they want all three of us to be in *The King and I*. Laura thinks it's because we were the only Asian kids, but I think we sang all right, too.

We learn to sing, "Getting to know you, getting to know all about you." We sway from side to side and pretend we're drinking little cups of tea, and then we giggle. We sit with our legs folded beneath us on the hard, dusty stage. I get to be the littlest princess because even though I just turned five Mom says it looks like I'm only three. I'm used to being the smallest one. At one part I have to crawl really fast between the King's legs. Then one of his guards picks me up right under my armpits. It hurts so badly I want to scream, but I'm supposed to "act" very cute and sweet and stupid like a little baby. Laura gets to be one of the Siamese twins, but her twin isn't Asian at all and they really don't look very much alike except they're the same height. Chet gets a speaking part. He yells, "Siam not so small!" at Anna during one of the lessons, but I think he should be the King's number one son. The boy they pick doesn't look Thai. He has red hair and his skin is peeling from sunburn.

Edward, the director of the play, likes his littlest princess, and I sit on his lap during rehearsals. He has a scratchy beard and he never yells even when Anna or the King mess up their lines and start laughing when they're supposed to be serious. Rehearsals get boring and I swing my legs from my perch on Edward's knee. I wait for the part when Tuptim sings and makes the hairs on my arms stand up. She's not Asian, but she is Mexican and I figure that's close enough.

Laura and Chet walk to Wendy's with their friends when we aren't practicing a kid part. They come back smelling like French fries and sipping on Cokes. They bring me a chocolate Frostie so I won't tell Mom they left me there all by myself. I have to drink it fast so Mom won't find out and the cold makes my head freeze.

After weeks of rehearsals, I have the whole play memorized. We get measured for costumes of sheer pink fabric and a sash draped over one shoulder. I wear makeup and Mom puts my hair up in a bun on the top of my head. She pulls and tugs on every strand until my eyes water. Then she sprays a cloud of Aquanet hairspray until the bathroom smells like a beauty parlor. Mom calls us her little princesses as we hop in the car and drive toward the theatre. During the play, I sing all the right words and crawl when I'm supposed to and I act cute even when the King's guard picks me up by the armpits. I love to watch Anna in her big dress. She floats across the stage when they play "Shall We Dance."

For the grand finale, we have to go see the King before he dies. My throat tightens as I watch his chest rise and fall, rise and fall. I know he's not really dying but I wonder what would happen if he really did stop breathing. I study the King's face, covered in powdered make-up; watch the wrinkles in his motionless skin. My knees hurt against the hard stage floor. I touch the sheets in the pretend-bed where the King is and remember Dad in the hospital, lying between real white sheets because his appendix almost burst. I think about Greg Bob lying in that coffin and I'm surprised when a tear rolls down my cheek, through my play make-up. They tell us we don't have to cry when the King dies at the end, but I cry every night.

After a while, I don't like being a princess very much. I'm tired of being the smallest. I'm tired of crawling through the King's legs and being picked up by my armpits. I wish Mitch were younger than me so I wouldn't have to be the baby anymore.

On closing night everyone acts sad and the King's wives give me hugs even though I barely know them. I'll miss the make-up and the costume and wearing my hair in a bun on the top of my head. When we're ready to go Mom carries me to the car and in the dim light of the parking lot she whispers that I stole the show.

After *The King and I*, Laura and I audition for parts in other local productions like *Alice in Wonderland* and *The Wizard of Oz*. Laura gets the good roles, even if they aren't the leads. She gets to be the Frog Footman and Toto, but she quits *The Wizard of Oz* because she doesn't want to play a dog. All of the leads go to the blonde girls, tall ones with blue eyes. I only get to be part of the chorus, or a munchkin, or a teapot.

KINDERGARTEN

Today I start kindergarten. Mom used to drop off Chet, Laura and Mitch at St. Francis while I stayed with her, but today I get dropped off too. I watch Chet, Laura and Mitch run through the double doors of the big brick building and turn down the hallway. Chet heads off to the sixth grade room, Laura to fourth, and Mitch to first. I watch their backs as they walk away from me and then Mom pulls me toward the black iron steps of the kindergarten room.

The steps to the basement are slippery from the morning dew and I wish I could be in the afternoon class with my friend Loretta who lives up the street. But Mom has a babysitting deal with two of the kids in the morning class and she won't change me.

I enter the classroom before most of the other kids arrive. Mom waves goodbye and my teacher, Ms. Christie, shows me a little rectangle of rug where I am to sit and wait. I watch the other kids come in. I don't know most of them but recognize a few from church. There's a little blonde girl with her hair in braids like Mary on *Little House on the Prairie*. I twist one of my short dark pigtails around my finger. A little boy in a navy jacket starts to cry when his mom leaves, which seems strange to me. I've been waiting forever to start school. He settles down after a minute and soon all of the little rectangles of carpet are filled.

Ms. Christie teaches us how to sing songs, paint and play. I like the peanut butter dough, the way it squishes and squeezes between my fingers and gets warm from my heat. When we're done we get to eat it and it tastes like peanut butter cookies.

I love to finger paint, too. I watch the wet color ooze from my hands and spread bright across my paper. I add more paint thinking it will get better and brighter but pretty soon it's just a big brown mess that I throw away.

There are blocks and tinker toys, but my favorite place to play is the sand box, which doesn't have sand. It's filled with cornmeal and smells like warm bread, which makes me hungry.

Our teacher, Miss Christie, waddles around our kindergarten basement. Miss Christie's nice, but I like her helper, Sonja. Sonja has the longest, blackest hair I've ever seen and she smiles way more than Miss Christie.

After school is over, I race to the white station wagon where Mom waits. I tell her how much I love school and we go eat ice cream because Chet, Laura and Mitch won't get out until 3:00.

Most days I'm early for kindergarten and Matt Rose is too so we play in the sand box. We drive Tonka trucks over hills we build with cornmeal.

After school I go home or to Matt or Allison's house to play. Matt can be mean, but he likes me better than Allison because she cries and tells on us if she doesn't get her way. Allison's mom buys her stuff from the Magic School Bus. It seems like she always has something new in the mail when we get to her house. I look through the Magic School Bus catalog and circle books and games I want. When Mom comes to pick me up I ask her if she'll buy me something. She says she'll ask Dad but she forgets and so do I until I'm back at Allison's house and she's opening another package.

At school Allison is quiet. Matt always gets in trouble because he is loud and shouts and runs. I wish I could get babysat with Willie Smith instead of Matt and Allison. Willie is nice. He shares and never teases me like Matt does. Willie's my best friend of all the kids in kindergarten, but I can't wait to start first grade so I can learn to read and stay at school all day long.

ON YOUR OWN

It's 3:00. Mom and I wait for Chet, Laura and Mitch to get out of school. In the rush of kids sprinting toward cars, I try to spot the dark heads of my siblings.

"It's been a year," Mom says out of the blue and I look at her face in the rear view mirror. "We picked up Mitch a year ago today."

I remember that day, how Mitch cried and I didn't want him to come home with us. I remember his red sweat suit and a strange smell but I can barely remember our family before Mitch came.

Mrs. Yaegar, the first grade teacher, walks toward our car and taps the window. I wonder if Mitch is in trouble. Maybe he did something in class and the teacher said, "I'll have to talk with your mother about this!" like Miss Christie sometimes says to Matt Rose. As I keep an eye out for Chet and Laura, I eavesdrop on Mom and Mitch's teacher. I hear nothing but good news.

"He's adjusting so well, such a nice boy, getting along just fine."

Miss Christie never comes out to tell Mom how well I'm doing.

"Hi, Nori." Mrs. Yaegar waves at me in the back seat. I wave back and try to smile.

Mitch climbs into the car and I slide all the way to the end of the seat. I pretend that if he touches me he might burn my skin. He's all smiles and holds papers with big red smiley faces on top. He hands them to Mom.

"Good job, Mitch!"

He says thanks and part of me misses the Mitch who didn't talk. Mitch smiles as he shows me his papers but I don't smile back.

Mitch doesn't need my help anymore. He doesn't need me to show him how to do anything or explain the rules or teach him how everything works because *he's adjusting so well* and *getting along just fine.*

Mitch, I decide, is on his own.

MOVING

After school, Matt Rose, Mitch and I crawl across the bunk beds in the boys' bedroom. We're making a spider web out of yarn, stretching and tying it to trap the bad guy. Mitch and Matt both have Spiderman Under Roos. I want Spiderman Under Roos too but they're only for boys. I'm wearing Wonder Woman Under Roos because that's what they make for girls.

When our web is complete, we turn off the lights and wait in the semi-darkness for someone to fly into our trap. We hear a knock at the door. I tell the boys to shhhhhh and reach to open the door. I pull it toward me and light streams in. The boys jump from the top bunk and scream. "Ahhhhhh."

We stop. It's Mom. "Time to clean up," she says flatly. "Matt, your mom's here," and she closes the door behind her.

"It is just too small," I hear Mom tell Dad that night. I've heard them discuss the size of our house before and remember all the times Mom yelled at us to go outside when Mitch and I ran through the kitchen too often. Maybe she's right. Maybe all Mom and Dad need to be happier is a bigger house. And more money. And fewer kids.

That weekend Mom and Dad start looking at houses. I go with them to visit a big two-story house on Revere that is so tall it reminds me of Noah's Ark. I imagine our family in every house we visit but there's something wrong with each one. Not enough bedrooms. Kitchen's too small. Driveway's too steep.

A few weeks later, on a Sunday afternoon, the whole family piles into the station wagon and drives up Shepard Road past the Charmichael's and the Garretson's. We turn down Revere and pull up to a farmhouse with the biggest yard I've ever seen. It is grey with white trim and an irrigation ditch runs through the side yard beneath a willow tree with a fort. Chet runs and jumps over the irrigation ditch and dares each of us to follow. Laura runs, leaps and makes it—no problem. Then it's either Mitch or me. I leap over the smaller ditch, just wider than a step for me, to measure how far my legs can stretch. I watch Mitch get ready to jump. He runs but takes off too early. His right leg slips back into the dirty water leaving his shoe stuck in the mud and the bottom of his jeans wet and brown. Mom calls us and Chet puts his arm around me. He walks me over the white-washed footbridge that spans the ditch and tells me, "You got lucky, Rod. Next time it's your turn."

I hope we get the grey house on Jones Road. I pray at church for three weeks and maybe that's the first time God answers me, because a week later Mom and Dad tell us we're moving. We pack our whole life into brown cardboard boxes.

I'm sad to say goodbye to the house on Shepard Road, to the Holly Hobby curtains in the room I share with Laura; to the trundle bed where I sleep, and the hallway I race down to be the first one Mom and Dad tuck into bed.

But I love the new house. It has two staircases, one on each side of the dining room. The staircase to the kids' bedrooms has tan carpet and at the top of those stairs a window looks into the backyard. Mitch and I share a room and Laura and Chet get their own. I feel rich in the new house and love sprinting up the steep steps to the kids' rooms where Mom and Dad rarely visit. I slam the door to the bathroom with no lock, and study the slanted ceilings of the bedrooms that mirror the roofline. Each room is unique, just like us. The other staircase leads to the playroom, an addition the previous owners built above the garage. The thin, teal carpet on those stairs carries you to a landing where the windows face northeast so you can see from our backyard all the way to the Ochocos.

After we settle into the house on Jones Road and explore the yard, one of the neighborhood kids visits. He lives in the big, new house across the street and is Mitch's age, but he seems much older. He comes over just as Chet, Mitch and I decide to check out the storm cellar. A heavy door on the backside of the house swings open to a steep staircase. It reminds me of the cellar in *The Wizard of*

Oz that Dorothy doesn't reach when she gets blown away to Oz. Mom says we don't have any tornadoes in Oregon but I'm glad we have a cellar just in case.

Chet heaves the door open and light pours into the darkness. We walk single file down the dust-covered steps and Chet pulls on a string connected to a bare bulb on the ceiling. The light is dim in the cold darkness and it smells like right before it rains. I look up at the cobwebs and exposed wood planks. Chet examines the water heater and I sit on a concrete step in a dim circle of light.

"You know, this basement's haunted," our neighbor announces as he makes sneaker prints in the fine dirt covering the cellar floor.

"Really?" Chet says, turning from the water heater.

"The previous owners said you should never come down here at night or the ghosts will suck the breath right out of you."

"I don't believe you," I tell him as I stand up to leave.

"Then you come down here some night. I dare you."

That night, when Mom says it's time for bed, I ask Chet if he'll go with me upstairs while I brush my teeth.

"You aren't scared are you, Rodriguez?"

"Just come with me."

Chet leans against the door of the bathroom as I brush. I can see him in the reflection of the mirror. "Don't worry about ghosts. There's no such thing. He was just trying to scare you. You want me to go back down to the basement and check?"

I spit into the sink, rinse the toothpaste off my brush and drink cold water right from the tap. I think about the dark, dusty basement and tell Chet, "No, it's okay. I'm not scared."

I jump into bed and Chet turns off the light.

"Night, Rod."

"Night."

He closes the door leaving me in the dark to stare at the shadows that crawl across the ceilings of our new house.

After a while, Mom starts to hate the house on Jones Road. She hates the always-peeling white trim. She hates the sound of our feet pounding up and down the stairs and how there's only one shower. She forgets how the house on Shepard Road was too small and remembers how great the long flat driveway was for riding bikes and how nice the trees were in the front yard. She blames the house on Jones Road for all of our problems, for costing too much, for being cold all the time, and for being too old. The sound of doors slamming replaces voices on silent afternoons and I miss sharing a room with Laura. The house doesn't make Mom and Dad any happier. And there's less money. And still four kids.

"We never should have bought this damn house," Mom says as she sits at the dining room table, paying the bills. "And we never should have bought this stupid table. I should have listened to your father."

The table is made of pine and holds every scratch, every dent. I look down and see impressions from Chet's math homework. I don't say anything. Mom's not talking to me. She's talking to God.

Dad says it's buyer's remorse, when you buy something and you wish you could take it back. I think back to life on Shepard Road, when it was just Chet, Laura, and me: before Mitch came. I wish I could go back to those days. I think Mom has buyer's remorse for lots of things besides the house on Jones Road.

GROWING UP PICTURES

Mitch and I help Mom unpack the last boxes from the move. We empty cardboard boxes marked "Family Room" in Dad's perfect all caps printing.

There's the box holding Mitch's shoes from when he first arrived, a red sweat suit and little rubber shoes that already look way too small to have ever fit Mitch's feet.

The next box holds Mom's wedding dress. Just like Mom's wedding ring, her dress doesn't look like any other wedding dress I've seen. It's creamy-white but short and straight instead of long and poofy and the thick, sparkly fabric reminds me of curtains. Then there are two little flowy dresses, sheer nightgowns Mom received as wedding gifts, one white, the other black. Mitch and I drape them over our clothes and dance around the family room like ballerinas. We can't stop laughing and I'm not sure Mitch understands how funny it is for him to wear a dress.

As Mitch and I spin in circles, Mom flips through a box of loose photographs. Mom and Dad's growing up pictures are faded black and white images of their parents and families. There is the wedding photo of Dad's parents, grandparents I never met, and then photo after photo of Dad's family: two parents with various combinations of their eleven children. I sit next to Mom on the floor and try to pick Dad out in each picture, "Is that him, Mom?"

She says, "No, no, no," and then, "yes, yes."

I notice the pattern. Dad is one of the youngest and he never smiles. I count all thirteen Nakadas in a shot taken from the farm and although I can't recognize the shadows of my young aunties and uncles from their Christmas visits, I can tell from age and height who might be Uncle Yoshio, Uncle Yoshinau, or Uncle Min. I have a hard time finding Uncle Sab and Uncle George because I've never met them, but Auntie Grace and Auntie Hannah stand out in their dresses. Then there are the younger boys, Uncle Jimmy, Uncle Steve and Dad. In every photo, from when he is a baby in his mother's arms, a little boy in overalls on the farm, to a teenager glaring from inside internment camp, Dad never smiles.

That same box holds Mom's growing up pictures too. She's the second oldest of four girls and I can easily sort Mom from her sisters. Even though Dad is ten years older than Mom, in these black and white growing up photos I can't tell that a decade separates them, or that the Barry's valley home sits only twenty miles from the Nakada farm. Mom's growing up photos don't have farmland or men in uniform. Her pictures have a manicured yard in the San Fernando Valley with little girls in pigtails sitting on ponies.

I ask Mom if life back then was in black and white and she laughs. "No, life is always in color."

Then, just like *The Wizard of Oz* when Dorothy gets scooped up from black and white Kansas and lands in Munchkin land, our family's history comes to life in color and lands in albums. The first album shows a young Dad, finally smiling as he stands in front of his bright red Austin Healy, and a young Mom decorating their first Christmas tree in Philadelphia. Then comes Chet, dressed up as a baby Santa, grinning toothless and then he's a toddler holding a frog. Laura comes next, first a pink bundle, then running in the green grass of the backyard and cooking at an EZ Bake Oven.

Mitch and I turn the plastic photo album pages. Our fingers graze the lives of our family before us. We wait, wait, wait to turn the page and see our own faces, our own history in the family collection.

I'm the baby laid across Chet and Laura's laps, and in Auntie Mitzi's arms when she and Uncle Henry came to visit from Alaska. There is baby-me when I got into Mom's makeup and cold cream and covered myself in a white mess. There's even a picture of me crying that Mom took because I so rarely cried.

Mitch sits silently beside me as I study these baby versions of myself and I wonder what Mitch looked like as a baby. Who looked into his newborn eyes? Who watched as he took his first steps or heard his first word? I look over at my brother who is here to stay, who won't be going back to Korea, who is now part of our family. I think about the first picture I saw of Mitch, before he was my brother, standing on a swing, not smiling. Mitch smiles all of the time now and I want to ask him what he remembers from Korea.

He might know the English words to explain, but Mitch doesn't say anything and I don't ask.

We reach the end of the album and the pages are empty. There are no pictures from when we went to the airport to pick up Mitch or from that first Halloween. Those are in an envelope that Mom says she hasn't had time for yet. I close the album and stack it on the shelf. It sits there next to the box of Mom and Dad's growing up pictures and the other albums of our family history waiting for what comes next.

PART TWO

NIGHTMARE

In the new house I wake up in the dark, crying. A bad dream. No monsters. Not falling or being chased by bad guys. In this dream, I'm alone. Mom and Dad are gone and it's just me and I have to find the keys to the garage.

I stumble downstairs to Mom and Dad's room. My head sits at the height of Mom's sleeping face. "I had a bad dream," I tell her as I shake her shoulder. She rolls over and I crawl into the warmth between my sleeping parents.

In the morning Mom asks me about my dream. She rubs my back and tells me it's all right. "But Nori, you're getting too old to crawl into bed with us. If you have a nightmare you can come tell me about it, but then you need to calm down and go back to bed."

I look at her and nod. Her head rests there on the pillow beside me and she looks tired. "I can't come sleep with you anymore?"

"Nope. You're getting too big for that."

"Okay," I say but I don't know if I can resist the warm coziness of my parents' bed.

I wake up in the dark. Another bad dream, but I'm not crying. I stumble downstairs trying to piece together the strange dark images into words I can tell Mom. I look at her sleeping face and I don't want to wake her. I whisper, "I had a bad dream." I go through the dream in my head, how I was trying to tie my shoelaces but the rabbit ear that was supposed to go through the hole wouldn't go and the laces became the ears of a squirmy rabbit. I tried to tie the laces again but the bad bunny started chasing me around a tree. The dream seems silly now and Mom's still asleep. My heart stops racing. I'm okay. It was just a bad dream.

I walk back upstairs and crawl into my cold bed alone.

FIRST GRADE

I'm finally starting first grade. Mitch is in second grade now, and I don't care if the other kids tease him about his accent. Sometimes I see him at recess, at the top of the slide, or on the monkey bars. He's always wearing that smile or laughing louder than all the other kids on the dodge ball court. Mitch is fine.

Laura's in fifth grade and Chet has moved on to seventh grade at Pilot Butte Junior High. With Chet gone, Laura is in charge of getting us to the bus stop every morning. Mitch and I know better than to be late. Chet can be mean, but Laura hits way harder.

It's cold in the morning when we walk up to Juniper Elementary, the public school, to catch the school bus downtown to St. Francis. The bus passes by our stop twice, once at 7:15 and again at 8:00. Laura makes us leave at 7:00 so we make the 7:15 bus. Then we get to ride the warm school bus on its route through town before arriving at school.

"Let's go," Laura yells as she stands at the door to the garage. I put my brown bag lunch in my backpack and follow Mitch out the door. Once we're on the road, our training begins.

"Run to the end of Jones," Laura orders. She's feeling like the oldest, like she has to pick up where Chet left off. She jogs down the road and I try to keep up. "Come on, Nori. Stop being such a baby. We have to make it on the first bus."

My legs and lungs burn from running in the cold. "I'm trying," I yell but it sounds more like a whine and I know Laura won't like that.

"Fine, we'll just sit in the cold for an hour because you couldn't run to the bus stop," Laura says, slowing to a brisk walk up 10th Street. I have to jog just to keep up with her.

Mitch hardly ever says anything but Laura says, "Come on, Nori," so many times that Mitch starts yelling at me too. He knows that I'm the youngest so even though he came later he can boss me around.

We make it up the long hill and we're almost to the bus stop. I have no idea how long we've taken. Laura and Mitch run up the last steep part but I just can't make my legs move any faster. Crossing the Juniper Elementary School playground, I wonder what it's like to go there instead of St. Francis. I study the tetherball and handball courts and imagine myself playing on the bars or swings. Then I hear my big sister again.

"Nori, hurry up!" Laura has turned to see where I am. Behind her, the yellow school bus pulls up. I hope Laura can catch it. I hope the driver sees us and stops so we don't have to sit and wait in the cold. If we don't catch it Laura will hate me because I'm so slow.

"Go!" I yell.

Laura turns and sprints over the last stretch of sidewalk with Mitch beside her. I make my legs run a few more steps and see Laura talking with the driver. I hope she tells her to wait for me, but the bus doors close and I imagine the bus pulling away without me.

I find the strength to sprint and the bus doesn't pull away. The doors swing open with a squeak and the bus driver looks down at me. She can probably tell I'm about to cry.

"I wasn't going to leave you, honey. I was just keeping in the heat."

I climb aboard the warm bus and sit next to Laura on the ride through town.

For first grade I have Miss Bartell. I wanted Mrs. Yaeger because Chet, Laura, and Mitch all had her when they were in first grade. Miss Bartell is a brand new teacher and having her is another way I'm different from my siblings.

On the first day I sit on the carpet, but I want to run across the hall to Mrs. Yaegar's room. Miss Bartell smiles and tells us she's from Wisconsin where her parents run a mink farm. I don't know what a mink looks like or what sound it makes. She tells us they use their fur to make coats and hats. I feel sad for all those little minks waiting around to be skinned.

By November, I love Miss Bartell. First grade is way better than kindergarten. My favorite time is Math Their Way. We do the calendar and put up numbers for yesterday, today and tomorrow.

We make patterns with different colored blocks. Pretty soon I see shapes and patterns in the ceiling, in the floor tiles, and in Linda Barncord's plaid skirt.

I also like reading. I'm in the Bears and we read from the second grade book because we're the fast group. Karen Thornton and Carrie Bland and a new boy named Daniel Callahan are in the Bears. Daniel Callahan used to live in California. His dad died and he and his mom and sister just moved to Bend. He is cute, cuter than Willie Smith who I used to like back in kindergarten.

Daniel Callahan already takes Communion and his mother goes to church every day. I wonder what she thinks about when she goes to mass in the middle of the week, when she's the only one there floating in a sea of empty pews. It's just her, the priest, and candles breathing through mass.

Every Friday, the students at St. Francis walk over to the church. It's just like mass on Sunday except students do the readings and the prayers.

One frosty morning I get to be a line leader and stand next to Miss Bartell. She's all bundled up in a fur scarf and a tube of fur covers her hands. She reaches out so I can touch it. "This is a mink muff," she tells me as we walk across the playground. She pulls the long scarf down for me to touch and I try not to think about when that fur was alive. I hold the thick mink in my bare hands. It feels softer than feathers, cotton balls and puppy ears all put together. It seems to hold its own heat and I wish I could crawl inside that muff of mink.

At Sunday mass, I look for Daniel Callahan. But I guess his family must go to the 10:30 mass and we are always at the 9:00.

Then, one Saturday, Mom says Daniel Callahan's mother is joining her bible study and I hope Daniel will come too.

Mitch and I play with Joe and Becky Butler in the front yard and when Daniel and his Mom climb out of their green car I show him the tree fort. I take him over the bridge to the apple trees in the side yard. We play tag with Mitch and Joe and Becky. I'm hot and sweaty and suddenly I have to go to the bathroom. I swing open the screen door and run to the downstairs bathroom. It's dark inside after being out in the sun and as my eyes adjust I push open the bathroom door. Before I can think to turn my head I see Daniel standing in front of the toilet with his jeans down around his ankles. He turns and looks right at me.

I take a deep breath, say sorry, back up and shut the door. All of the blood in my body pours into my face. "I won't tell anyone if you don't," I yell at the closed door.

The only sound I hear from the bathroom is the toilet flushing.

I sprint up the stairs to the other bathroom, slam the door and pull a drawer open so no one can get in. I hide in the bathroom until all the moms say goodbye, back their cars onto the street and drive away.

SOCCER

When I start playing soccer on a real team I'll get a uniform. I will be number ten like Pelé, the greatest player in the world. Chet wears ten, and Laura and Mitch do too. Before soccer starts at Marshall Park on Wednesday afternoons, I practice dribbling in the front yard. Dad tells me not to look down and to kick the ball with the inside of my foot, not my toes. I end up kicking air and leaving the ball behind me at first. I start to get better and Dad tells me to keep my arms straight; to stop running like a girl.

At soccer practice I am the only girl besides Ali, but she doesn't count because she hates soccer and running. Laura is usually the only girl on her teams so it doesn't bother me. I practice dribbling, passing, and shooting. I keep my arms straight. I run after the ball with the boys.

We've had five games and I still haven't scored a goal. That's all Chet and Laura want to know when they ask about my games. "So did you score?" I always have to tell them no.

Today is the last game of the season and we're playing Matt Rose's team. Matt always scores for his team.

Earlier this week Matt said, "We play you on Saturday, Nori. We're going to beat you. You think you can score on me?"

I gave Matt my meanest look and said, "We'll see."

It's a sunny fall morning at Marshall Park. The sky is cloudless and blue except for a few wisps of smoke rising from the chimneys of houses near the park. I have my uniform on, number ten, and shin guards and cleats. The frost on the grass hasn't melted and crunches with each step. It's my last game so Mom, Dad, Chet, Mitch and Laura have come to watch. I keep my eyes on Matt during the first half. He runs around just like he does at school but here everyone claps instead of yelling at him. He dribbles fast and kicks the ball hard. I'm not scared of him though.

Matt scores in the first half and so does a boy on my team but no one has scored in the second half and the refs are about to blow the whistle to end the game.

I get the ball at midfield and feel someone chasing me from behind. I dribble as fast as I can down the sideline, my cleats digging into the grass and dirt.

The whole world bounces up and down as I run and breathe and try not to look at the ball. In front of me, all I see is green grass and the goal.

From the corner of my eye, I see Matt pulling alongside me. I can out run him, but I push the ball a little too far in front of me with my left foot. It's rolling out of bounds, but then Matt slides, trying to steal the ball. His body skids in front of the ball and he somehow keeps it from going out of bounds.

The ball is back at my feet and I have only the goalie to beat. I sprint, shoot for the far corner and watch the ball dance into the back of the net. The crowd cheers from the sideline and my teammates surround me. Mom, Chet, Laura and Mitch smile and give me hugs and then Dad lifts me into the air.

Matt Rose lies on his back by the sideline. After the game Matt gives me a high five but he isn't smiling. He doesn't talk to me until after Christmas.

DUKES OF HAZZARD

Mom doesn't like us watching the *Dukes of Hazzard*. She says it's unrealistic to have all of those car crashes and then show people walking away without a scratch. She also doesn't like how the cops are stupid and those "good ol' boys" always get away. She doesn't like the Duke boys' car either because it has the Confederate flag on the top. Somehow that means they are racist.

But Mitch and I like watching that show and I like Luke Duke. He has dark hair and grey eyes. Most of the girls in my class like Bo Duke because he looks like a Ken doll. I also like how Daisy Duke has brown hair instead of blonde. I get the feeling Mom doesn't like Daisy Duke though because she hates it when I tie up my t-shirts like Daisy does.

Mitch and I play hide and seek in the backyard. He counts from the willow tree, which is home base, while I run to hide behind the woodpile by the back porch. I can barely hear him counting. He gets to twenty and peeks out from the side of the tree. I try to keep an eye on him but can't see him when I hear a strange crash and Mitch starts yelling. He shouts so loudly I know we aren't playing hide and seek anymore. Mitch still has a strong accent but I can tell he's saying something about the *Dukes of Hazzard*. I run to the willow tree and there is a car right there in our backyard. Mitch shows me with his hands and crashing sound effects how the car jumped from the road, crashed through the fence, and landed between two apple trees. We run to the house to tell Mom. I try to explain but Mitch just keeps saying, "*Dukes of Hazzard, Dukes of Hazzard!*" Mom doesn't believe us until we pull her to the backyard and she sees the car sitting there.

Mom herds us inside and calls the police. She keeps hugging and kissing us both repeating, "My god, he could have killed you."

With Mom's arms tight around me, I remember Greg Bob lying in his casket, and for just a second, I imagine Mitch or myself lying lifeless beneath the branches of the willow tree. Sirens blare from outside and Mom lets us go.

Mitch and I run upstairs to Chet's room to watch the police and ambulance from the window. They pull a man from the car and he looks like he's okay as he stumbles toward the ambulance. Mom talks to the police by the front door but I can't hear what they say.

Mitch keeps saying, "Yee haw!" just like those Duke boys do when they go flying down the dirt roads of Hazzard County.

BEING A GIRL

I hate being a girl. I hate dresses and shoes that hurt my toes. I hate how they paint girl bikes pink and put ribbons on them and make the bar in the front lower. I hate how boys can play with their shirts off but I can't. I hate how the boys at school think I won't be any good at kick ball so they never pick me until all the other boys have been chosen. That's when I kick the ball high over their heads and they scurry across the playground while I run the bases. I love being smaller than all of them and faster and smarter.

Before church every Sunday, Mom picks out a dress for me to wear. They are never new dresses, maybe new hand-me-downs, but never *really* new. Some are ones Laura wore or they're from the Van Slykes, the ones Brenda's grown out of. I don't really care what I wear to church on Sunday but I don't like certain kinds of dresses. I want dresses like the ones Laura Ingalls wears on *Little House on the Prairie* with small waists that you tie into a bow in the back. I don't like the ones Mom thinks are so cute: baby doll dresses. Those make me look fat and I hate wearing them.

This Sunday, Mom makes me wear a dress she knows I hate. Laura says I'm acting like a baby so I put on the stupid dress. I cross my arms in front of my chest as we walk into church. As we fill the entire pew I decide I hate my family. I hate how there are so many of us, and how we always sit at the front of the church. I hate that we never, ever, leave mass early and how Mom sings off key. I hate how our family doesn't seem to look or act like anyone else in this town. And I hate my dress.

QUITTING

Mom isn't skiing this year. Last year Dad forgot to lock the rack and one of her skis fell off the top of the car and down the steep mountainside where it was impossible to retrieve. Mom decided it was a sign from God that she should stop skiing.

I wonder how Dad feels about Mom quitting. Dad never quits anything.

Mom and Dad fell in love skiing. There are pictures of them when they were dating, standing on slopes together, holding their skis in front of lodges in Utah or Colorado. Mom wears a black ski jacket and looks so thin and young and happy. Dad's smile gleams from his tan face and his hair is shiny black instead of salt and pepper grey.

I loved the feeling of riding in the car last year with the whole family piled in warm and cozy and snow falling all around us. Now it's just Dad with all four of us kids on the mountain. I don't like to think about Mom at home all day by herself while we're skiing, but when we get home, I stand in front of the fireplace to warm my bones, and Mom brings out cookies she made while we were gone. The house smells like the chicken noodle soup with rice she knew would taste perfect after a cold day on the mountain. Soon I forget how Mom complained about her legs hurting and how cold it was. I forget how she looked leaning into her turns on the mountain or pulling off her parka in the lodge. I forget that Mom ever stood on a mountain at all.

FLARE-UP

Mom hasn't been feeling well lately. She's sore and tired. She goes to the doctor and they tell her she has arthritis. They give her pills to help the pain and swelling. Sometimes Mom's fingers puff up so big she can't wear her wedding ring.

I try to figure out what causes Mom's flare-ups, when she rubs her hands together like she's washing them because the joints hurt, and she moans as she gets up from the couch. Sometimes the flare-ups come when it rains and I wonder if Mom is dying because she stays in bed all day. On other days, when it's sunny and the sky is perfect and blue, Mom's joints get so stiff she can't shift the car into reverse without my help.

Then, like magic, Mom feels better. She starts a new medication and it works. She smiles again and has energy to take Mitch and me for a drive.

On hot summer days Mom likes to take afternoon drives with the air conditioning on. There was a forest fire south of town a few days ago so Mom takes us to see it. We listen to the radio and head down highway 97. We turn right onto a small dirt road and the radio fades to static. Mitch and I sit in the back seat, looking out the windows at the towering pine trees.

In a flash the forest turns from green to black. Mom drives slowly on the soft dirt road where there are no trees, no chipmunks, no sagebrush. There is nothing alive at all. We are the only car on the road, driving where the fire just burned through and smoke rises from the ground where trees used to grow. The car starts to smell like fire and Mom turns the air conditioning down. We don't talk. We just stare at a world that looks like the inside of a wood stove.

"How did it start?" I ask mesmerized by the destruction.

Mom isn't sure.

"Are you sure they put it all out?" I imagine our car surrounded by an unexpected flare-up just like when Mom can hardly get out of bed and it hurts for her to stir oatmeal in a pot or flip pancakes on the griddle.

"Yes, Honey. I'm sure they put it out," Mom tells me with a certainty she never has when she talks her about her arthritis. Mom turns the car around. She puts the car in reverse, and I watch her from the back seat, shifting from reverse to first, reverse to first, fearing the next flare-up.

MONEY

Mom sits at the dining room table surrounded by piles of paper. She has a calculator and a photocopy of *The Budget*. I looked at it once. It's a big chart in Dad's handwriting listing everything we need each month and how much it costs. Mom writes and erases and I can tell she's getting frustrated because every breath is a sigh.

When I hear her yell, "John!" it's trouble.

I sprint up to the TV room so I won't have to hear this month's fight. Whenever Mom and Dad talk about money it gets bad. Mom usually starts to cry and Dad tells her not to worry. Mom says, "We never should have bought this house," or "If the car breaks down again what are we going to do?"

After the monthly budget fight it's hard to ask for anything extra like new shoes or money to go to 7-11. I don't think that kind of stuff is on *The Budget*. Maybe Mom and Dad plan these fights so we won't beg for stuff like some kids do.

I come in from playing outside and walk into the kitchen for a glass of milk. Mom has us drink powdered milk because it's cheaper than real milk. I don't notice the difference except at the bottom of the pitcher when clumps of powder make the milk thick and gooey. Today the pitcher is full so I pour myself a glass. Then I see this brown, wooden box on the counter. "What is this thing?" I ask Mom.

"It's our new flour mill," she tells me.

She and Dad read this book called *Sugar Blues*. It's about how bad sugar is so Mom and Dad have decided that our family will cut out all refined sugar. Mom says white bread is nothing more than sugar so she's going to bake whole wheat bread and grind her own flour.

I don't think it's about sugar, though. It's really about money or Mom's arthritis. I'm sure it's cheaper to make your own bread than to buy it and maybe sugar is what makes Mom's joints hurt. We already do all kinds of things to save money, like timing our showers in the morning to save water, and Mom will try anything to make her arthritis better.

The next day our house smells like a bakery. Mom's bread pans are in the oven and I turn on the light to take a look. Loaves of bread bake inside, turning a golden brown. I ask Mom if they're ready yet because if that bread tastes anything like it smells, it's going to be delicious. Finally, Mom pulls the loaves out, cuts me a slice and spreads butter on top. I sit in the breakfast room, my feet dangling from the chair, nibbling on warm, homemade bread.

Money is tight all over Bend. The city stops running the school bus route to St. Francis so on the first day of second grade Mom has to drop Laura, Mitch and me off.

At lunchtime, our class walks over to the cafeteria. We sit at the second grade table now. I look at all the new lunch boxes: Matt's Empire Strikes Back lunch box, Stephanie's Strawberry Shortcake lunch box, Richard's A-Team lunch box. Matt has a roast beef sandwich, chips and a Capri Sun. Stephanie has a peanut butter and jelly sandwich on white bread cut in half diagonally, and a thermos full of apple juice. Richard has string cheese, raisins in a little box, apple slices, and Oreo cookies.

I have a brown paper bag. Matt laughs about something and I'm sure it's my lunch. I open my bag to a peanut butter and honey sandwich on Mom's homemade bread and a banana. I pull out the sandwich and it breaks. The only thing holding the bread together is the peanut butter and honey. Homemade bread tastes delicious right out of the oven, but once it cools it becomes a dry, dense mess. My sandwich falls apart as soon as I take it out of the plastic baggie. I know no one will want to trade for anything in my lunch, so I sit and try to eat my sandwich. I chew and wish for a thermos full of real milk instead of powdered, and a sandwich on plain, old white bread. I wish I had a new lunch box and that just once in a while I might find a cookie or a bag of chips inside. I pick at my sandwich until all I have is a bag of breadcrumbs.

PRAY

I don't know what that tightness in my chest is, but I'm sure I'm dying. I felt it once in kindergarten, but it went away. In first grade it happened again so I took deep breaths and even though it felt like my heart was going to burst, it passed.

I pray when I'm trying to fall asleep at night, after I say an Our Father and a Hail Mary.

I pray that I won't die. I don't want to die yet.

I pray that Mom's arthritis will get better.

I pray that we'll win the lottery and have all the money we need.

I pray that Mom and Dad won't get a divorce.

I pray for a puppy.

I pray for all of the poor and sick people.

I pray that no one in my family will die like Greg Bob.

Please, God, in Jesus name.

But for every prayer, I imagine the opposite.

I imagine what would happen if I died or if Laura or Chet or Mitch died.

I imagine Dad losing his job so we're even poorer. We never get a puppy, and the poor stay poor and the sick stay sick.

Mom and Dad get a divorce and I have to choose between them like in that movie *Kramer v. Kramer*.

I cry silent, salty tears in the dark of my bedroom, until sleep rescues me.

WISHING FOR SNOW

At sunset, the world grows cold and dark. The red line of the thermometer outside the kitchen window creeps from 34 degrees to 33. I watch the line drop toward the magic numbers: 32 degrees Fahrenheit, 0 Celsius. It hits 32 and then keeps dropping until it rests in the mid-twenties. Now it is certain. Anything that falls from the dark night sky will be snow.

I look up into the starless sky and wish for a couple of white inches to cover the ugly, dead of winter, the naked tree branches, the brown grass, and the frozen asphalt so everything will look fresh and clean again. The clouds will break and the sun will shine through the clear, cold air. The snow will sparkle as if the whole world is sprinkled with diamonds, such a brilliant white that my eyes will hurt and I will be torn between looking out at the perfect snow and wanting to play in it, to cast snow angels and bring snowmen to life. The next night I'll wish for more snow, enough to cover the imperfections we created that day, to fill in the snow angels and bury the snowmen because even they will look more beautiful covered in a new layer of white.

"Nori, time for bed!"

I've been staring out the window for an hour and still no snow. I head upstairs, climb into my cold bed and shiver until the sheets warm up. I try to fall asleep but since counting sheep never helps I force my mind to wander through starry skies, away from all the things I should have prayed for. I travel past galaxies and planets and into the vast nothingness of a black hole, and if I still haven't fallen asleep, I sit up and look out the window, hoping that instead of darkness, I'll see millions of white flakes falling like stars from the sky, turning my ugly world perfect and white. Most of the time the world remains dark, barren, cold and dry, or just a trace of snow dusts the trees and rooftops. I wake up morning after morning wishing for more.

MITCH AND MOM

"Look at me when I'm talking to you."

That is what Mom says to Mitch all the time. I wonder if that is their biggest problem. Is that why Mom gets so mad at Mitch all of the time? I can't put my finger on it. Why does Mom yell at Mitch more than me? She seems so much less patient with him and I don't know why, but I think it has something to do with Mitch's inability to look her in the eye.

TV TIME

Mom and Dad get all kinds of crazy ideas about raising us. First, they moved to Bend instead of bringing us up in LA, where they both grew up. In Bend, they joined St. Francis church and I think that's where they get most of their crazy ideas.

First there is the fighting. If we hit one another, or shove, or punch, we have to donate a quarter to the poor box at church.

Then it's swearing. Same idea. The four shits Mom says while making dinner equals a dollar.

The worst, though, is their newest idea.

I stare at the yellow clock in the breakfast room that matches the yellow striped wallpaper. It's Sunday and the clock says 2:02. We've already gone to church and it's time for our weekly family meeting. I drum my fingers on the table and wait. I'm always the first person here. Mom comes in and tells me to go upstairs and get my brothers and sister. I drag my feet to the bottom of the stairs and yell, "Family Meeting!"

I sit back down at the breakfast room table and wait. Mom holds a spiral notebook. I wonder what that's for.

Once everyone is at the table we talk about the upcoming week. Mitch and I don't have much to say but Laura and Chet have basketball practices and games.

After we check in, Mom tells us we're going to start having TV time. "Each of us gets to choose two hours a week of TV to watch. You can watch one another's choices too. That adds up to 12 hours a week which is a lot of TV."

I look at Mitch. This is going to be hard for us. We have a whole after school line-up. We watch *Transformers*, *GI Joe* and *Scooby Doo*. Those three shows on one day would blow most of our minutes. Mom passes around a spiral notebook. "This is the TV log. If you turn on the TV, just to see what's on, that's okay, but if you choose a show to watch you have to record it in the log."

I look at the top of the page. Mom has already written: name, start time, finish time, and total minutes. I think I might want to spend my time on Saturday morning cartoons but I don't tell anyone. Maybe Mitch will choose it too and I'll just watch his TV time. Chet doesn't say anything. He rolls his eyes at the idea and so does Laura, but Laura hardly watches any TV so she doesn't really care. Dad doesn't say much either. No one really says much at family meetings so they're over fast.

I end up using up all my minutes that day because *Swiss Family Robinson* is the Disney Sunday Night Movie. The rest of the week is quiet without the buzz of the TV in the background. I listen for anyone walking up the stairs to the family room and when I do I sprint to see if someone is planning to watch TV so I can join them.

TV time only lasts a few weeks. It's not because we're driving Mom and Dad crazy. It's not because people cheat. Mitch and I have been watching that log and keeping track. It's just that Mom and Dad can't follow the rules. Mom likes to watch *MASH* after she makes dinner. Dad can't even watch a whole football game with two hours. Then *Roots* starts. Mom and Dad want to watch every episode and it's on a bunch of nights in a row so they suspend TV time indefinitely. None of us argue.

WAITING

The asphalt outside the house on Jones Road is dark. A car's headlights shine across the street and into the ponderosa pines. They point up over the hill and send shadows stretching across the road. I watch for our station wagon, for headlights that turn into our driveway, followed by the hum of the garage door opening.

I'm not sure where Chet, Laura and Mitch are, somewhere watching TV or reading a book. They don't care that Mom and Dad are late, that they said they'd be home around 7:00 and it's now 8:00. Where are they? I picture the twisted metal of a car accident, our white station wagon wrapped around a tree like a broken toy.

Another car's headlights shimmer across the asphalt, glow into the tree limbs and speed past our house.

My chest tightens and I start counting. I figure that by the time I get to one hundred, they'll be home. One, two, three... I reach one hundred. Two cars have passed by and they still aren't home. I'm holding my breath. I feel like I've been holding my breath ever since I noticed Mom and Dad were late. I make myself take deep breaths.

What if they never come home? If Mom and Dad are dead will they split us kids up? No one wants four kids, not all four. Would Mitch and I stay together or would they send the boys to one family and the girls to another? One time Mom said that if anything happened to them we would all go live with Auntie Grace and Uncle Sat in California. I know some of my other cousins went to live with them after Uncle George committed suicide. He died before I was born and I can't imagine what it would be like to not want to live.

Another set of headlights.

I might not want to live if Mom and Dad never come home, or if they get a divorce and I have to choose one of them.

Footsteps pound down the stairs and Laura opens the door from the bedrooms. "What are you looking at?"

"I'm waiting for Mom and Dad. They're late. They should be home by now." My voice quivers even though I try to sound calm.

Laura can tell I'm scared. She puts a warm hand on my back. "It's okay, Nor. They'll be home soon."

We stare out the window and for a second, instead of seeing out the window, I see Laura and me, our straight, dark hair and faces glowing in the reflection of the glass. We look the same in the dark glass. We stay like that for a minute, with her hand on my back and right when I start to believe her, headlights light up the ponderosa pines and this time the car slows and the headlights turn into our driveway. The garage door opens and Laura says quietly, "See, they're home."

PING-PONG

For Christmas this year Grandma and Grandpa give Mom and Dad a hundred dollars to buy something for us kids. Mom and Dad talk about it for a while and decide on a ping-pong table. Dad, Chet and Mitch drive out to GI Joes in the truck to pick it up. It takes a couple of hours, but pretty soon the table is set up and ready to go.

It's hard to get used to the way the little white ball bounces. Holding the paddle makes Mom's hands hurt so she gives up and it's up to Dad to teach us. Before long, we get the hang of it. We each grip the paddle a little differently and have our own style. Dad holds the paddle with his index finger and thumb right along the base. He played ping-pong when he was stationed in Alaska with the Army. He moves quickly behind the table and hits the ball hard. Chet holds the paddle a lot like Dad except his index finger is further out. Laura has a tough serve and she's consistent. She counts on you to make mistakes. Mitch has quick hands and is good with both his forehand and backhand. I am okay. I line up far on the left side so I don't have to hit my backhand and my serve is decent but I hardly ever serve an ace.

We play games to 21 and once a rally gets going, there's a rhythm like a clock—tick, tock, tick, tock, tick, tock, until the clock breaks and a point is won. The best shots are when the ball just nicks the edge of the table because there's no way your opponent can get it.

Chet says we're having a ping-pong tournament. "Winners play one another, and then the winner is the Nakada family champion."

Mitch and I play first. It's close but Mitch makes a couple of slams and starts laughing. I hate it when he does that. I try to slam it back but keep over-hitting and the ball flies through the air past the end of the table. Mitch wins 21-13. Then Laura and Chet play. It's a good match, but like our game, Chet pulls away, not because he's all that good, he just keeps talking and it makes Laura mad. On every point Chet has something to say. "Oh, too bad," or, "Tough shot, tough shot." Chet doesn't let up with Laura or Mitch. When he plays me, he knows he's going to win so he says, "Good try, Rod," or, "You've gotta work on that backhand." With Laura and Mitch it's always pure celebration. "That sure was fast. Did you even see the ball?" or he just yells, "Yes!" Chet doesn't play chess anymore, but he definitely plays ping-pong. Chet wins the tournament. He is the Nakada Family Ping-Pong Champion.

When friends come over they're really excited that we have a ping-pong table. I wonder if our friends think we're good at ping-pong because we're Asian, when really it's just because we're the ones who have a table.

Mitch gets tired of losing to Chet. I'm lying on the couch watching cartoons.
"Wanna play ping-pong?" Mitch asks.
I'm sick of losing, too. I never beat anyone at anything. "No, that's all right," I tell him.
Mitch pushes one end of the table up against the wall and practices behind me. Tick, tick, tock, tick, tick, tock, miss. I watch *The Smurfs* but I can still hear Mitch and after a while it sounds like he could hit the ball forever. I watch a whole cartoon and Mitch is still playing. I bet Mitch will be able to beat Chet pretty soon.

After a while Chet and Mitch are the only ones who use the table. Sometimes Laura and I play with our friends but they are so bad it's no fun because you can't get a rally going. We occasionally play doubles, Mitch and Laura against Chet and me. It's usually a close match and then someone gets mad and quits before we finish.

I retire from family tournaments even though Mitch tries to coach me into being a better ping-pong player. I can't make that little white ball do exactly what I want it to and I'm sick of losing. After that first winter, the ping-pong table begins to gather dust. The big green table and red, foamy paddles asks to be played, but we wish we had an Atari instead.

SIN

"Bless me Father, for I have sinned. This is my First Confession."

We all repeat after Miss Van Domelyn. I squirm in my chair, look at the snow falling outside the windows of our second grade classroom, and try to get the words to stick in my head. This is what I have to say to the priest at my First Confession and I don't want to forget. Miss Van Domelyn tells us we might get nervous so for homework we have to think of our sins and practice what we're going to say to the priest after "Bless me Father, for I have sinned."

Carrie Bland asks, "What if you can't think of a sin?"

She asked that same question yesterday and I can't believe she's asking again. Miss Van Domelyn reminds us that we have to think back over our whole lives. I'm sure I've sinned. Seven years, all those commandments. I was okay on all of the big ones. I haven't killed anyone and I don't think mosquitoes count. I only pray to one God even though he's divided into three parts. I've never stolen anything. I never use God's name in vain. I've missed the Sabbath a couple of times and I was jealous of Daniel Callahan's Vans because they were the exact ones I wanted—the black ones with black and white checkerboard around the bottom—and that's coveting thy neighbor. I don't think I've lied except for the time I ate flour but didn't want Mom to find out or when I hid my green beans in my napkin and threw them away instead of eating them. I could confess that, but the commandment Miss Van Domelyn keeps talking about is "Honor thy father and mother." I'm not sure what it means to honor them but I think it's a sin when I get mad at Mom and slam the door. I'm sure it's a sin when I don't pray for Mom and Dad to be happy before I go to bed at night.

After mass that next Sunday I notice the confessionals at the back of the church: the doors with shiny knobs, and deep, dark wood. I wonder what it's like inside and what sins those walls have heard, the grown-up sins that Mom and Dad might have, the ones that really count.

I hope I get Father Kelly. I wish Father James was still here, but he's at a church in San Francisco now. Father James used to pop his false teeth out and play soccer at church picnics in his brown Franciscan robes. But since I can't have Father James, I'll take Father Kelly. He's been here longest. Mom doesn't like him though. Sometimes after mass she says, "I can't believe Father Kelly said that." I try to think about what he said but I can never remember anything that would make Mom upset. Father Kelly is still better than Father Ken whose face is always red. He looks like his phone connection to God might not be so clear.

On the cold morning of our First Confession we walk to the church in our winter coats, hats and mittens. There are no fancy dresses or suits like a First Communion and there will be no family waiting at the end of mass to go to brunch. First Confession is not that big of a deal. Our two lines are quiet. I guess we're all thinking about our sins.
I walk and stare at the white puffs of breath appearing and disappearing before me. I count all 15 stairs up to the church and Mrs. Van Domelyn opens the tall doors. It's dark and quiet inside except for our footsteps. Our two lines split off to separate sides of the church. We genuflect, in the name of the Father, the Son and the Holy Spirit and kneel down. I bow my head and let my eyes adjust to the dim light filtering through the stained glass windows. I wonder which priest is in the confessional behind me.
Daniel Callahan goes first in our line. He went to Catholic school in California and already did his First Confession and First Communion. We wait in the quiet of the church and I listen hard. Is it a sin to try to hear someone else's sins?
The confessional knob clicks and the door squeaks as it opens and shuts. I look down the line. Six people before my turn. Each time the door squeaks open I want to look over my shoulder to see if my classmates look any different when they come out. I try to guess how long each confession takes by counting one alligator, two

alligator, three alligator. The longer the confession the more sins, right? Karen Thornton takes 31 alligators.

Matt Rose stands up and turns back to confess his sins. I wonder what he will confess. Will he mention how he makes fun of my lunch in a brown paper bag instead of the cool metal *Empire Strikes Back* lunch box he has? I listen to his footsteps as he walks toward the confessional. I try to hear what he says but it all sounds like people talking underwater. Matt Rose doesn't stay very long and before I can count to 20 alligators it's my turn.

I walk toward the dark wood, twist the shiny knob and open the door. My hands are sweaty. I can't see anything for a second. Then there is a wood seat and a closed window in the dark booth. The door shuts behind me with a click. It smells like Lemon Pledge, soap and cigarettes. I sit down and a dry hand slides the window open.

"Bless me Father for I have sinned. This is my First Confession." My voice doesn't even sound like me.

The priest says a jumble of words so fast I can't understand them. It's not Father Kelly. It's Father Ken. My face turns hot and I can't remember any of the sins I planned to say. I tell him I lied to my parents. He says something back to me, a loud whisper that I am sure everyone sitting in the pews can hear, but all I remember is my penance. "One Our Father and two Hail Marys."

I leave the heat of the booth and wait to feel cleansed. That's what Mom told me. "You feel a weight lift. Your sins have been absolved."

I don't feel any different. I just feel hot and sweaty like I'd been trapped in that little box forever. I say my one Our Father and my two Hail Marys as fast as I can so no one will know my penance even though you aren't supposed to talk about it. That is between God and me.

FAIRY TALE

Cody French invites me to his birthday party. I'm the only girl invited and Mom isn't sure she wants me to go. But Laura was in Cody's sister's Girl Scout troop so Mom decides it's okay. The French family has a hot tub, so I'm supposed to bring my swimsuit.

At the party, I'm embarrassed and climb quickly into the hot, bubbly water. We start talking about school and the boys all say I'm the coolest girl in our class. My face turns red and maybe it's because of the hot tub, but as I sit in a cloud of steam and the boys talk about the 49ers I never forget that I'm a girl. Even though I play sports, hate wearing dresses, and wish I were a boy most of the time, I'm still a girl.

Sometimes I flip through the pages of the Disney picture book in secret. When Mom sends me to pick a book to read before bed I can't choose that Disney picture book. The first time I picked it she said it wasn't a *real* book, so now I only look at it when I'm alone in the family room. I turn past the story of Snow White and her dwarfs, past Sleeping Beauty and the evil queen's mirror, mirror on the wall to my favorite fairy tale: Cinderella with her stepsisters, and her fairy godmother turning mice into horses so Cinderella can go to the ball.

This past summer I woke up super early to watch Princess Diana get married in the biggest, most beautiful wedding in the world. Mom must have noticed because on Christmas morning I unwrapped a box holding a bridal doll wearing a white ball gown just like the one Cinderella would have worn to her wedding. She has perfect blonde hair tied up under a long veil. I twirl my doll and imagine her waltzing across a dance floor to, "Shall We Dance?" from *The King and I*.

The story of my parents' wedding is like a fairy tale. Dad got a job offer in Philadelphia and asked Mom to go with him. She agreed and quit her job the next day. That weekend permissions were granted, rings purchased and Mom and Dad married on a Wednesday night (after bowling league) before a crowd of family and friends.

I look at their thick white wedding album in secret just like I do with the Disney picture book. Mom is healthy and thin and beautiful. She wears a knee-length white dress and a little pillbox hat with a flyaway veil. Dad wears a dark suit and thin tie. Beneath his jet black crew cut is his smile, a smile I've seen in real life but never in any of Dad's growing up pictures.

There is the altar with Mom's sisters on one side and Dad's brothers on the other. There is the kiss and the smiling couple coming down the aisle. There is the rice tossed into the air and cake placed delicately in one another's mouths. There is a long-distance phone call to Uncle Min because he lived on the east coast and no one called to tell him Johnny was getting married. There is the last picture in my parents' wedding album, before they move to Philadelphia and then back to LA, before Chet and Laura are born and they move to Bend, before they have me and adopt Mitch. In that last picture my parents look out the back window of a car. The window is foggy with excited breath and the bride and groom smile. They look out the back window before driving off to live happily ever after.

I don't talk about fairy tales or weddings to anyone. I'm not a princess, or a bride and there are no fairy godmothers. I talk about the 49ers and the Trailblazers. And when we get out of the hot tub at Cody French's birthday party, I go to the bathroom to change into my jeans and t-shirt because I'm still just a girl.

PUTTING UP A FIGHT

In our house you fight like Mom or you fight like Dad.

If you fight like Mom there's yelling and screaming. You sob and slam doors and scream. If you fight like Mom you say things you might regret later like, "I hate this family," or "I'm running away," or "I wish you weren't my mom." It feels really good to say it in the moment, but if you say things like that and slam doors as you storm out of the house you might have to really run away, and then you have to hope someone comes after you to convince you to stay. You have to go back and apologize later.

If you fight like Dad, it could last days or weeks because you don't say anything. It might even take a few days before someone notices you're fighting with them. You sulk, and glare and shake your head. You only answer yes or no to questions, or you just shrug. You have to be patient to fight like this and let the anger brew inside. This kind of fight either fades away as you forget why you are mad, or it explodes into a Mom-fight. It depends who you're fighting.

Chet and I yell and cry and slam doors.

Laura and Mitch glare and pout and say nothing.

It's a Sunday afternoon and the house sits in a heavy silence. The weight of it feels like a Dad fight brewing. We're heading toward the explosion of a Mom fight but you never know when it might happen, or if there really is a fight beneath all of the silence.

Dad works outside in the garden and Laura reads in her room while Mitch and Chet watch baseball turned down low so they don't bother Mom. She sits at the kitchen table doing the bills. I'm lying upside-down on the couch with the funny pages, blood rushing to my head, trying figure out the Doonesbury joke. I wait for a break in the silence, some sound that will allow me to ask Mom about the cartoon like a car rushing past or the phone ringing. A sound.

Something. Anything. And then it comes, like a car crashing though the picture window.

"John!" Mom yells and before I can turn invisible, somersault off the couch and escape to my room, she spots me.

"Nori, where's your father?"

I shrug even though I know he's working outside.

"Go find him."

I fall off the couch with a thud and trudge through the thick silence of the living room, past the dining room table littered with bills, budgets, and Mom's open checkbook, into the kitchen, through the utility room, and out the back door.

The wind blows through the long branches of the weeping willow and a flock of geese pass overhead. Dad leans over a row of string bean seedlings. His olive green overalls disappear as he bends down, immersed in the tall grass of the field.

"Dad!" I yell, but my voice disappears on the wind. I hop down the steps and walk toward him until I'm standing right next to him, his face sweaty and dark with dirt. He looks up at me, wrinkles forming around his eyes as he squints into the weak spring sunlight.

He grins. "Hey, Noriko."

"Mom wants you."

His smile vanishes and a gloved hand pushes his dark hair from his forehead. "Tell her I'll be there in a minute."

I turn back to the house. Mom stands at the window facing Dad and me. I can't read her face in the glare of the window. A cold gust of mountain air rushes across my face as I walk back to the house.

Inside it feels stale and stuffy. There's the smell of the beef stew Mom started after church and silence surrounds the tick tick tick of the yellow clock in the breakfast room.

"He said he'll come in a minute," I tell her and wait. She doesn't say anything. She washes rice at the kitchen sink. Her wedding ring glints on the windowsill. I walk back to the living room, and notice the table is cleared of bills and budgets.

The silence finally breaks when Mom calls us to dinner. The noise of our family crashes around the table and the silence lifts as we hold hands and say grace.

PROBLEMS AT HOME

Every Monday the kids at St. Francis Elementary gather in the hallway and sit on the floor for morning prayer. They turn the lights out so it's dark and Sister Jane lights a candle. She leads us through an Our Father and Hail Mary, and then she prays for the Lord to help us learn and obey our teachers. We pray for people who might be sick. We pray for teachers and their families. We pray to St. Francis who was a friend of animals and children. Then Sister Jane asks if anyone needs a special blessing.

I sit with my legs crossed in front of me and try not to think about this morning when Dad walked into the kitchen and said, "You kids make sure you pray for us at school today."

I was just finishing my cereal when Mom chased in behind him, "No, no, no." She talks to us but glares at Dad. "You don't pray for family problems at school. We're fine. No one's getting a divorce."

I stared as Mom noisily unloaded the dishwasher and Dad silently packed his lunch. They said nothing else and Laura, Mitch and I left for school just like any other day.

I wonder if Laura and Mitch think our family needs a prayer, a special blessing so our parents stay together. I don't say anything and neither does Laura or Mitch, but when Sister Jane asks us to say our own prayers in our minds, I bet all three of us pray for the same thing.

The next weekend Mom and Dad send each of us to stay with a different family. I want to stay with the Ellises but Mitch gets them. Instead I stay with the Ericksons, a family we barely know from church. Chet stays with the Corrigans and Laura with the Hurleys. I'm nervous to be all by myself because the Ericksons don't have any kids, but they have a big shaggy St. Bernard like the ones that carry barrels through the snow in cartoons.

Mom drops me off at their house on Friday night and Laura gives me a big hug as I get out of the car. When I look back at her she looks like she might cry. I wish I could go with Laura instead of staying here. Then she could explain what's going on. She would make this sinking feeling go away.

Before I know it I'm inside a strange living room and when the front door closes with me on one side and Mom on the other, I start counting the minutes until someone comes to pick me up.

I think about Mom and Dad going away together and wonder what they do when they're alone. It must be boring not having any kids around. I worry that it will be silent, like a Dad fight, but I'm even more worried that things will explode into a Mom fight and they'll decide to separate. If that happens I might have to stay in this house with no kids and a smelly, hairy dog sleeping and slobbering all day.

On Sunday morning, instead of going to church, I lean against the dog and watch football while I wait for Mom and Dad to pick me up. I know they'll come. I try not to think about Laura's eyes welling up and tell myself, they'll be here. It feels worse than waiting for the first day of school or to open presents on Christmas morning. They'll be here soon I keep thinking and before halftime Dad's at the door. He lifts me up, "*Yosho*!" He holds me tight and carries me away from that house and its hairy dog.

We pick up Chet, Laura and Mitch, and head home. Mom makes lasagna and I'm so happy we're eating dinner on a Sunday afternoon just like usual that I almost forget the sinking feeling I had on Friday.

I watch Mom and Dad for a sign that everything is okay but it seems like nothing has changed. I hope things are better even though I can't see it. That would mean my prayers worked.

TRADING FAMILIES

The Garretsons go to St. Francis and they have five kids. Ray, the oldest, is friends with Chet, and Loretta, the youngest girl, is in my grade.

Loretta and I play with her Barbies in the room she shares with her sister. She tells me her mom is going to have another baby.

"Just think," I tell Loretta as she takes a pair of scissors to Barbie's hair. "If your Mom has a boy, your family will be just like *The Brady Bunch*: three girls and three boys." I don't tell Loretta how I've also noticed that she has blonde hair like Cindy Brady instead of dark hair like mine.

"Yeah, that would be neat but I want a little sister to play with."

Loretta already has a little brother but they never play together. I wish I had a little sister, too, but it would be better to have three boys and three girls like the Brady Bunch. I make her a deal. "If you get a little sister, you can keep her, but if you get a little brother, I'll trade you families." We shake on it.

Just before Loretta's mom's due-date she's in a car accident. The brakes go out in the Garretson's station wagon and it plows right into someone's living room. Mrs. Garretson gets thrown from the car, but she lands so the baby isn't hurt.

Mrs. Garretson has a baby boy so the Garretsons are like *The Brady Bunch* and Loretta is like Cindy.

We never trade families but I wish my family could be more like *The Brady Bunch*. The Brady kids have fun together and I wouldn't even mind being the youngest because Cindy gets included in the band. Her brothers and sisters play with her even though she whines. Chet and Laura are too busy to spend time with Mitch and me. They hate going to family meetings or doing anything with us. If I could trade families, I would definitely go to *The Brady Bunch*.

JAP

Chet's in the eighth grade and instead playing with us he hangs out with his friends. They come over to play football or wiffle ball in the backyard. I know better than to ask to join them. Chet doesn't let Laura or Mitch play so there's no way he would let me. I watch them play 500 from the breakfast room where I can see the entire yard. One boy throws the football and then the other boys try to catch it. If you catch it on the fly it's worth one hundred points. If it bounces or someone else touches it, it's worth less.

Ray Garretson, Scott Green, Ron Lowe and a couple of other boys I don't know push, shove, run, catch and throw. As they laugh and smile I wish I was older, and a boy.

Chet's school calls one afternoon and tells Mom she needs to come pick up Chet. He got in a fight.

"Chet, you are *never* to get in fights at school. What's the matter with you?"

Chet doesn't say anything. He looks at his feet.

A few weeks later Mom gets another call. Chet was in another fight. When Dad gets home that night I stand with Laura and Mitch at the top of the staircase so we can hear. Mom talks about how violence doesn't solve anything and only makes things worse. She asks Chet why he got in a fight again and Chet says something I can't hear. Next thing we know Chet is walking up the stairs. The three of us run into Laura's room and wait for Chet's bedroom door to close. Then we hear Mom and Dad yelling.

"What do you mean you told him he could?" Mom screeches.

"They called him a Jap. It's the one thing he can fight for."

I think about all of Dad's growing up pictures, not a single smile. I remember when Dad first came home from internment camp. He got kicked out of a high school football game for fighting.

Jap. I've never heard this word before but Laura says it's like the N-word for Japanese people. I've seen it in a thick book of black and white photographs about the camps. On the cover there's a little girl holding a suitcase with a numbered tag wrapped around a button on her black coat and inside there are pictures of stores with signs saying, *No Japs!* or *Go Home Japs!*

The next day after school the TV blares in the family room. Laura pretends to watch for a minute before turning to me. "I found out what happened with Chet yesterday." I look at her but her eyes are on the TV. In a voice so quiet I can barely hear, Laura tells me "Jared called Chet a dirty Jap. Chet told him to take it back but he wouldn't so Chet hit him."

I think back to the boys all playing football in the backyard. "I thought Chet and Jared were friends," I tell Laura.

"I thought so too, but I guess not."

That night, I wait to fall asleep and hear Mom and Dad talking about what happened with Chet again.

"Sue, you just don't understand," Dad's voice sounds like he sucked on a helium balloon. "I didn't think things like this would happen here. I didn't think our kids..."

"Things aren't like they were when you were a kid. There's no war and no one is being sent off to a camp."

"I thought things had changed." Dad's voice is back to normal now. "But some things never change. *Shikataganai.*"

It's quiet then and I don't understand what Dad means. Maybe it has to do with being a boy. There are different rules for boys than girls. Lying in bed, staring into the dark, I think being a girl might not be so bad.

CALIFORNIA

Every second of the drive to California for summer vacation feels heavy, weighted down just like our car, packed tight with the six of us, suitcases stretching at their zippers, and the big cooler stuffed full of snacks. Dad drives the station wagon along cool mountain passes, past Lake Shasta and down into a desert valley where the sky is clear and the hot sun pounds through the windows. There is nothing to see except hills that look like blankets thrown over sleeping giants. I watch for something to change but nothing has looked different for hours.

We play games to keep busy. We look for license plates from all 50 states and have 36 so far; even Hawaii and Alaska, the ones we thought would be the toughest. We play the alphabet game so many times we don't want to play anymore. Mom made us stop playing slug bug when we were still in Oregon.

Mitch sleeps in the way back and Chet, Laura and I sit in the backseat trying not to touch one another's sticky, sweaty bodies. I'm hungry but Mitch ate all the Ritz crackers.

Chet keeps farting and laughing. Laura rolls down the window to get rid of the smell, and adjusts her pillowcase in the window for shade.

When we start climbing the Grapevine, Dad has to turn off the air conditioning. I try not to think about the heat and picture those California Raisins singing "I heard it through the grapevine," but I think this grapevine is supposed to be an actual grapevine and not a bunch of people telling stories that get messed up like when you play telephone.

The sun falls behind the hills and cars speed across eight freeway lanes. I've never seen so many cars and I can't check all of the license plates to see which states they're from. We pass Magic Mountain's huge roller coasters reaching into the blue sky and Chet asks if we can go on those rides but Mom says we're too close to Aunt Bev's to stop now. We're too close and the car sags with the weight.

We change freeways and exit in Chatsworth where we'll stay with Aunt Bev, Mom's older sister. We pull up to her house and park next to several cars already there on the lawn. I step out of the car, my legs unsteady from sitting for so long. I stretch and stumble toward the front door where Aunt Bev waits to hug us. The sun has set, but the air is heavy and hot.

Our cousins Marc, Scott, and Traci wait inside where it smells like cigarettes and animals. All of the doors and windows are flung open begging a breeze to pull in off the ocean and cool things down for the evening. Craigor, who used to live with us, watches the Dodger game in the dark of the living room.

Chet and Mitch join Marc, Scott and Craigor in the glow of the TV. Marc tells Traci to get him a soda from the fridge. I follow Traci into the kitchen and then we go outside with Laura to play with the dogs. Traci talks about her horses up at the ranch and I dream of riding with her someday.

The next day Aunt Bobbie and Aunt Patti come over and the weather gets even hotter. Aunt Patti brings her two kids, Sean, who looks like a surfer, and Michelle, who looks like a real valley girl. Sometimes Mom calls me Patti because Aunt Patti is her baby sister and I'm the baby in our family.

Stories bounce and rattle around the living room, and I can't tell Mom's voice from her sisters'. They talk about Grandpa's health, Grandma's heart, the new apartment in Encino, and what Uncle Al or Aunt Marian said the other day. I struggle to match names to faces like I can on Dad's side of the family, but we don't see Mom's side every year like we do with the Nakadas. On Mom's side of the family it's Aunt Bev, Aunt Patti, Aunt Bobbie and never Aunt*ie* Grace or Aunt*ie* Jo or Aunt*ie* Ginny like on Dad's side. But that's not the only difference.

Mom and Dad let us do things at Aunt Bev's that they never let us do at home. We stay up late, drink soda and watch rated R movies. In California the rules from home are gone. In this house anything goes.

Marc's girlfriend comes over to watch movies and she has long blonde hair just like you'd think a girl from California would. All my cousins look like that, blonde hair and tan, even in the winter. Chet and our cousins laugh at the jokes in *Repo Man* that I don't get and Laura glares at the screen so I figure the jokes must be dirty.

I have no idea what's happening in the movie so I go to the bathroom. I sit on the padded toilet seat, wash my hands with the little pink soap and then gaze into the mirror. I run my fingers through my long brown hair, lighter from long summer days and hours in the pool, but there's not a streak of blonde. I smile and catch a glimpse of my mother, maybe Aunt Patty or Traci in the reflection. Someone knocks on the door and Traci pushes the door open and washes her hands at the sink. In the mirror Traci's straight blonde hair turns mine even darker and any resemblance I'd imagined a moment ago fades away. I sneak past Traci out of the bright light of the bathroom and disappear into the dark family room.

Aunt Bev drinks beer and smokes. Mom and Dad never drink or smoke. Never. Never a glass of wine at dinner. Never a beer with pizza. Mom and Dad don't smoke. Not cigarettes like Aunt Bev, Grandma and Grandpa. Not cloves like Marc. Dad used to be an alcoholic and Mom told him if he got drunk again she'd leave him. Dad never drank again. Mom used to smoke but when Dad refused to buy her another pack, she quit cold turkey.

We go to the beach the next day and I walk with Laura and Traci to the playground. They play on the only two swings and their laughter floats on the salty air. They talk with one another and ignore me so I decide to head back.

I look for the green umbrella where Mom, Dad and the rest of the family are, but all the people blend together. The hot sand burns my feet as I search the crowded beach but I can't find them. I start to cry and I'm not sure if it's because my sister didn't care that I left or because I'm lost. I start planning to walk back to Oregon even though I can't remember all of the freeways. I'll walk up the coast and then head east.

A woman in a purple bathing suit sees me crying. She takes me to a lifeguard and I climb up the tower to look for my family. I still don't see them. The lifeguard makes some calls and I sit on the edge of the lifeguard stand waiting, my legs dangling above the crowd, the sand and the sea.

Mom picks me up. She has to drive because I walked so far. Laura and Traci get in trouble for letting me wander off by myself, but I don't care. At least I won't have to walk all the way to Oregon.

Marc and Scott take us to Disneyland. It's hot. The lines are long and my legs are tired from all that walking at the beach. We stand in long lines at The Haunted Mansion, Matterhorn and Space Mountain, and I don't even see Small World. That's the only ride I remember from my last trip to Disneyland.

On our last night in California, Aunt Bobbie and Uncle Lyle, Aunt Patti and Uncle Lynn, Grandma and Grandpa, Great Uncle Al and Great Aunt Marian come over, and then, because we don't have time to drive into the city, Uncle Steve and Auntie Jo, Uncle Yosh and Auntie Suma, Uncle Sat and Auntie Grace come over too. The cigarettes and beer cans of Mom's family collide with the Hawaiian shortbread cookies and *senbei* crackers of Dad's family.

Uncle Sat and Uncle Yosh play five-card stud with Grandpa and Uncle Al. My aunties take over Aunt Bev's kitchen just like they do when they come to our house, but instead of being annoyed like Mom gets, Aunt Bev seems grateful. The boys watch the Dodger game and play wiffle ball in the backyard while Traci and Laura flip through magazines with pictures of Ricky Schroeder and Menudo.

A collision of white and brown, blonde and black flows from the house onto metal folding chairs and plastic lawn furniture on the patio. Chet, Laura, Mitch and I occupy a strange space somewhere in the middle. We play with the dogs, watch TV and move in and out of conversations between Mom and Dad's two worlds.

The heat wave breaks sending a cool breeze through the valley. I watch games played at portable card tables and listen to tales from both families of jobs and layoffs, sports and movies, but never a word about politics or religion. I remember from that first Christmas Dad's family came, when we still lived in the house on Shepard Road, that we don't talk about differences. No one mentions that Mitch is adopted, that Chet, Laura and I are neither white nor Asian but something in between, or that none of Mom's sisters went to college and all of Dad's brothers did. No one says anything about Mom being ten years younger than Dad so that during World War II, while Dad's brothers fought overseas and the rest of the family withered away at camp, Mom and her sisters played hopscotch. In this backyard, there are too many differences to mention.

I lie on a plastic lounge chair in the backyard and look up at the night sky. I watch for falling stars but they hide behind the bright lights of the city. Every so often I hear Mom's laugh or Dad's deep chuckle weaving between the voices of their families.

I used to wonder why Mom and Dad moved away from LA, away from both of their families to a distant place where the stars don't hide in the lights of a city sky. I didn't know why they would want to start over in a mountain town where no one knew them or their two very different worlds. On a summer evening, deep in the heart of the San Fernando Valley, I begin to understand my parents' decision.

Tomorrow we'll get in the car and drive away from the weight of this city, leaving behind the sweltering heat and dirty brown skies. We'll pull away from this house; pass by forests, mountains and lakes until we reach the thin, light air of Central Oregon.

In Bend, Mom and Dad found a place where they could create their own family. In Bend we know who we are.

SUMMER BALL

I hop on my bike and pull the leather strap of my baseball glove over the handle. Today I have baseball practice and Mom says I have to ride my bike.

I stand on the pedals and pick up speed to make it over the grass and up the driveway. I turn left on the dirt road, dodge potholes, and pull up on the handlebars at the spot where the asphalt starts. They just paved this road and the sweet smell of tar coats the dry summer air. I coast down Thompson Road and know I'll hate this hill on the way home. If we still lived at the house on Shepard Road this ride would only take two minutes. Now that we live on Jones Road it takes five.

The fence along the outfield at Stover Park is covered in bushes so instead of looking like a fence it looks like the ivy at that old ballpark in Chicago. I drop my bike by the first base dugout and pull my glove off the handlebars. Some of the same boys who were on my soccer team are there and I'm the only girl. I've gotten used to that though, and since Chet makes me practice in the backyard I could be better than lots of the boys.

Our coach pulls up in an old VW van. He asks us our names and we pair up and play catch. Coach puts us at the different positions and I want to play shortstop. That is where the best player always is. Chet is a shortstop and Laura too. Mitch plays the outfield though because he has a great arm. We don't get to hit, but Coach says we will at the next practice.

I'm jealous of all the boys whose parents pick them up while I hop on my bike to ride home. The sky is perfectly blue and I stand up on the pedals to get up the hill on Thompson.

When I get home I drink water straight from the sink, and then lie on the couch to watch baseball on TV.

PETS

Mom and Dad always come up with plans for making money like when they opened up a Catholic bookstore. This time they plan to get a purebred dog and sell her puppies. They figure that will shut us up about getting a dog and they'll make money.

We drive toward Redmond and down a long driveway to where a yellow lab just had puppies. In the yard of a farmhouse there's a green tent holding more puppies than I've ever seen. I try to count them but they squirm around and it's hard to keep track of all those little yellow heads and tails. They smell warm and moist and are so tiny. They crawl and stretch over one another and whimper.

Goldie is the runt of the litter and when we take her home I sleep with her in the utility room that first night. She cries and I feel sorry for our little puppy who used to sleep in a warm green tent with her brothers and sisters and now she's stuck with just me. I rub my fingers on her soft ears that remind me of mink until we both fall asleep.

I want Goldie to love me more than anyone else in the house, but as she gets bigger, she becomes a handful. Chet takes Goldie to dog obedience classes and she tries to attack the other dogs. Every once in a while, someone leaves a door open and Goldie makes a run for it. She sprints across the Riemer's yard, jumps the ditch and ends up at the Nicholson's dog kennel, barking at their two pointers. Goldie would never hurt a person, but with other dogs, she barks and growls and bears her canines. I can see blood in her eyes. She wants to kill.

I don't have the patience or the strength to handle Goldie when she reaches adult size and then we find out she has a chemical imbalance that makes her aggressive. We have to keep her on a leash all the time and only Dad and Chet are strong enough to take her on walks.

A couple of times we take Goldie to the river and she gets to play off leash. She runs at full speed, her muscles flexing and pulling beneath her thick coat. She leaps into the river and swims against the strongest currents. Then she climbs out and shakes, spraying water in waves that sparkle in the sunlight.

Early one morning, the neighbor's little black terrier gets out. When Mom opens the screen to get the paper Goldie charges out the front door and is on that dog fast. Mom hits Goldie with the newspaper and then her broom but Goldie's sharp Labrador teeth sink deep into that little dog. Goldie shakes him, trying to break his neck. Chet races out, grabs Goldie by the collar, and squeezes her jaw until the dog drops to the ground.

We have to pay the vet bills but the little black terrier is okay.

Goldie is not. Mom and Dad talk about what to do with her. "Maybe if there weren't so many dogs in the neighborhood or if we lived further out or built a fence."

I think about my cousin Traci. A German Shepard bit her last year and she needed 18 stitches and plastic surgery.

Mom and Dad decide Goldie must go. Just like Mochi before her, Goldie is gone and I never see her again.

The Duncans give us a cat. They don't want him because he peed all over their bed. After loosing Goldie, I'm happy to have a pet again.

We name him Neko. *Neko* is what they call cats in Japan, little white and black cats with red ears and collars that wave hello from store windows and bring prosperity. Neko is grey and white and his tail is just a little nub. Neko makes himself at home and poops in Dad's toolbox. I think Neko will have to go after that, but Dad lets us keep him.

Neko sleeps in the garage and he's not the brightest cat. He curls up under the tires of the car because they hold heat. Mom usually checks before she backs out of the garage, but one day she forgets and runs right over Neko. The car breaks his leg but Neko has nine lives so he survives. From then on, Neko sits on the steps of the porch with one leg hanging off to the side like it should be in a cast.

Neko explores the neighborhood and because he's not so smart he ends up at the Duke's house. They have a German Shepard and Neko climbs a tree in their yard to get away from him. Too bad that tree is home to a family of blue jays. They poke and prod Neko but that stupid cat won't come down. Eventually, Mitch climbs up and carries Neko out of the tree. That is when Neko becomes Mitch's.

Neko blows it when he poops in Mom's slippers. He goes to a family from church and we hear Neko is up to his old tricks again. He pooped in Mr. Ellis's work boots. I'm sure we'll hear about Neko for a long time. Neko will never die.

THIRD GRADE

In the third grade I have Mr. Bassett. I hear he's mean and he used to be in the Army. I've never had a male teacher and last year Mitch had to miss recess for almost a month because he couldn't memorize his times tables.

Once third grade starts it's not so bad. I learn to write in cursive and memorize my multiplication facts, which is a lot like adding, but faster. I pass all of my times table tests until we get to the nines and I can't get the numbers to stick in my brain. I have to stay in at recess and I've never missed recess before.

Karen Thornton stays in with me. She teaches me a trick counting the nines on your fingers so I don't have to miss recess.

I still like Daniel Callahan. He is cute and we both like Devo. "Hello, this is Devo. We would like to say things go both ways." He has black and white-checkered Vans and to impress him, I ask Mom for Vans for my birthday. We go to a store and order the exact ones I want. They are blue and white-checkered. When I wear them to school Daniel says they look cool.

I write my first story called Cherry Crunch Land. It's about a whole town made of my favorite dessert. I read all ten pages in front of the class and Matt Rose tells me to write a shorter story next time. I tell him to shut up.

In third grade I learn that at school, I can forget all about home. I can forget about Mom and Dad fighting, or Mom being sick or whatever might be going on with Chet, Laura or Mitch. At recess Mitch and I ignore one another and when we pray at assembly on Mondays or in mass on Fridays I don't think about home. School is my place to forget all about everything that's happening in the grey house on Jones Road.

For a whole week I have flag duty and it's my job to put the U.S. and Oregon flags up in front of the school. A couple of fourth graders show Matt Rose and me how. "Don't let the U.S. flag touch the ground or else we have to burn it," they say. They teach us how to fold the flags into triangles and show us the shelf in the principal's office where we leave them at the end of the day.

I'm worried about having flag duty with Matt. He goofs around a lot and I always feel like I'm going to get in trouble when I'm with him. On Monday we pull the flags down. He takes one end and I take the other. Everything goes perfectly.

"You didn't think I could do this, huh?" Matt asks me. "I don't mess everything up."

I shrug as I carry the folded flags to the principal's office. I think back to the time Matt cheated on the spelling test and when he ran away from home. "Yeah, I know," I tell him.

Tuesday things are fine too but on Wednesday Matt is absent so Karen Thornton helps me. Thursday Matt's back and he asks me how things went yesterday. I tell him Karen wasn't as good at folding as he is.

On Friday, Matt is hyper. He gets in trouble at mass and has to sit in a pew by himself. At 2:30 we leave to take down the flags. Matt runs through the hall to the drinking fountain. I walk slower than usual.

We get to the front of the school and when I pull down the Oregon flag everything goes fine, but with the U.S. flag Matt reaches up and says, "Oh, no. I think I'm going to drop it." He looks at me with fake panic.

"Knock it off, Matt."

"I'm just joking."

Matt unclips the flag and I grab the end dangling in the air. We each hold a side and snap the stars and stripes between us. Matt starts waving his end. I grip my end tight so the flag doesn't fly away.

"Come on, just fold it."

Matt looks at me and then tosses his end into the air. I stretch as high as I can to keep the flag from touching the ground but I'm too short and the bottom flutters down the steps. "I hate you, Matt! You ruined it."

"Oh, stop." Matt grabs the end and we fold the flag. He tucks in the end and I push the flag at him. "What's your problem?" he asks. "Why are you always so serious?"

"You let it touch the ground."

"No, I didn't," he snarls. Matt turns back into the school with a smile and I say nothing.

We walk back to class as if nothing ever happened and no one notices a difference. No one knows the flag touched the ground. No one else knows our secret, but I remember every time I walk past the flagpole.

WHEN MOM IS SICK

At church on Sundays we pray for people in the parish who are sick and need the Lord's help. I wonder why all God's miracles happened such a long time ago. Why did he help them back then, but not us now? Still, I pray. I kneel in church every Sunday as we pray for Mrs. Edwards. She has two little boys and cancer. We pray for Mrs. Reynolds, the fourth grade teacher who has a tumor in her leg. We pray for their doctors and families.

Prayer at church is for other people. When Mom and Dad were thinking about getting a divorce we never prayed for them and when Mom gets sick, the church never prays for her.

Mom stays in bed. Her hands swell up and she can't cook. Dad tries to make spaghetti but he puts cayenne pepper in the sauce instead of regular pepper and it's so spicy none of us can eat it. Laura and I try to make turkey tetrazini but we use a whole cup of chicken bouillon instead of putting the bouillon cubes in water. It ends up being so salty that we have to drink a whole glass of water between bites.

The doctors don't know what to do about Mom's arthritis. She takes medicine that makes her fat. She is tired all of the time and she can't get out of bed on bad days.

I can't figure out why the church doesn't pray for her. Maybe Mom doesn't want them to know she's sick. But if she told them, then they would know why she's gained all that weight, why she doesn't help out at the potlucks, why we always go straight home after mass instead of to the Parish Center for coffee.

I walk into Mom and Dad's bedroom to see if Mom needs anything. She's in bed facing the television. *MASH* is on and Hawkeye Pierce drinks a martini. I wonder why Mom likes *MASH* when she hates people drinking. I think about asking her but Mom's not really watching the TV so instead I ask if she needs anything. She shakes her head and I watch a tear slide down her cheek.

I try not to yell in the house or slam the doors when Mom's not feeling well, but sometimes I forget. I run down the stairs to answer the phone and shout, "I'll get it!" I slam the bathroom door, forgetting that Mom's in bed. When I do stuff like that Mom yells at me from the bedroom and I think I should remember to tell the priest about this at my next confession.

Sometimes Mom feels worse when it rains. Sometimes cold days and clear skies are bad. Then there are weeks at a time when Mom doesn't seem sick at all. Maybe the people at church *are* praying for her.

On bad days, I run from our car, down the sidewalk, and into my classroom to escape. I forget how quiet it is at our house and how it smells like sickness. Instead I think about the spelling bee or the school musical. When the bell rings for us to go home I walk down the sidewalk and forget about the tissue paper stained glass art project in my hand. I look for Mom and wonder if she'll feel well enough to cook dinner tonight.

THE JENSEN'S POND

The Jensens own the field behind ours where they graze two horses. Sometimes Laura and I take carrots or sugar cubes, sit on the top rail of the fence and wait for the horses to trot over and eat from our palms. Their warm lips tickle as they gently nuzzle the treats from our hands and let us pet their noses.

The Jensens have a pond by their stables. Mitch and I crawl between logs of the fence and under barbed wire to get from our backyard to the Jensen's. The pond water is murky and the bottom is covered in muck.

In the spring we catch tadpoles in our palms and sometimes they are already becoming frogs with legs pushing out from their squirming bodies.

You have to watch your back if Chet is at the pond. He'll catch you off guard and push you in. Your sneakers will get sucked into the mud like quicksand and you'll have to take your shoes off and dig through the muck to get them out. Mitch gets it the most because he forgets to keep track of Chet.

In a cold snap the pond freezes over. At first there's a thin layer of ice and snow and even though it looks solid you can fall right through. After a week of really cold days, the ice gets thick and we wonder if we could skate on it. Laura, Mitch and I walk across our snowy backyard with skates slung over our shoulders. We crawl under both fences, jump the dry ditches and stand at the edge of the pond.

"You're the lightest, Nori. Go first to see if it will hold," Laura orders.

I set my skates down on the snow, excited to be the one chosen to lead this expedition. I study the crust of the pond. It looks solid so I ease one foot off the bank and onto the frozen water. My breath puffs out hot before me. I put a little more weight on my foot and pause to see if the ice gives. It holds so I slide my other foot out. Okay so far. I inch out further clearing strips on the ice where my sneakers have pushed away the snow. Inch by inch, I make my way further from shore. The ice lets out a creak beneath me. I look back to Mitch and Laura standing on the snowy bank.

"I don't know," I say back to them. "I don't think we can skate on this."

"You're almost to the middle. Just get across." Laura yells.

My heart pounds and I imagine the water beneath me where frozen fish stare with wide eyes into the slushy water. It's so cold down there that if I fell through and got trapped I could drown and freeze like all those fish. I take a tiny step and the ice snaps like bones breaking. A lightning-shaped crack spreads from my foot.

"You're right in the middle; that's the weakest part. See if you can jump to the other side," Laura shouts.

I want to tell her she can try jumping to the other side but instead I keep inching across; watching the crack to see if it spreads. Bumps in the ice push against the soles of my shoes, and I try to gauge just how far it is to the shore. It looks pretty close, so I take three steps as lightly as I can, and leap to solid ground. "I made it," I say in a whisper and then turn back to Mitch and Laura on the other side. "Come on, Mitch!"

"No way. It cracked with you."

Mitch and Laura grab the skates and head back to the house.

"Maybe in a couple of days we'll try again," Laura tells us, but the weather turns warm the next day. The snow melts, and the Jensen's pond turns back to water.

FIRST COMMUNION

I never have new clothes. Everything I put on smells like my sister or my brother, or the Corrigans, a family from church with a million kids. Everything I wear has been worn before, molded to someone else's knees, someone else's body. These clothes have already climbed trees, gone to birthday parties, and watched cartoons on Saturday mornings. I put on a green shirt, not new, but new to me, and it takes a few weeks before it becomes mine, smells like me, feels like me.

I used to want a white dress for my First Communion, but Mom says white is for my wedding day and this is not my wedding day. Loretta gets to wear white, but not a veil. I'm sure Carrie Dolynick will get to wear white and a veil. At The Shalom Shop, the Catholic Bookstore where Mom works when she's not sick, there is a section behind the Thomas Merton books with First Communion dresses and veils. They are wrapped in stiff plastic that cracks when you touch it. They are so white they look blue in the florescent lights. I touch the bright, plastic-covered tulle and imagine myself looking like the little girl in the picture, but then I hear Mom coming. If she sees me wishing for a white dress and a veil it will make her feel bad so I move to the jewelry section and pretend to look at the rosaries.

Mom and I shop for my First Communion dress at the Bon Marché in the Bend River Mall. I stand at the rounder of dresses and breathe in the new clothes, something I've only smelled in stores. Today that smell is coming home with me. I finger the plastic hangers, slide the yellow, pink, and lime green dresses along the metal pole. There are baby blue dresses with flowers and yellow ones with ribbons but I want a purple dress. No, not purple, light purple. Laura says it's called lavender. Lavender. Mom pulls dresses that are purple or navy. "No." I tell her, "That's not really lavender." I finally come to a dress with a white lace petticoat and tiny white flowers on a field of lavender. I think it's perfect and when I try it on, it fits. It's my dress. It even says Cinderella on the tag.

The Friday before my First Communion we go to confession so we will be pure for our First Communion. I like how after confession I feel like a crisp white sheet of construction paper or a perfectly erased chalkboard. With all my sins wiped clean, I'm careful not to sin all day.

On Saturday my new dress waits on my bed, clean and perfect. Mom curls my hair and gives me two barrettes with shiny white and lavender ribbons. I put on my dress and even though the lace is scratchy, I feel beautiful. I walk down the stairs to look in the full-length mirror in Mom and Dad's room. I clasp my hands in front of me and twist in front of the mirror, watching my dress and hair swing from side to side.

At church, my classmates and I sit in the front pew. I like my dress better than everyone else's, even the white ones. Only Carrie Dolynick has a veil so it's okay that I don't have one. I read the First Letter to the Corinthians and don't make any mistakes.

When it is time, I go up to take Communion and try not to get grossed out when the priest says, "This is the Body of Christ," and places the stiff, white wafer in my hands. I put the host in my mouth where it melts on my tongue. "This is the Blood of Christ." I sip of the sour wine and avoid thinking about all of the other lips that have touched that gold cup.

I kneel back down at my pew and watch the rest of the congregation file forward. Mom and Dad, Chet, Laura and Mitch all take Communion like the rest of the church. Then someone's little sister stands before the priest. She isn't even old enough for kindergarten and she holds her hand on her heart so the priest knows she hasn't had her First Communion. The Father recites a blessing and the girl turns to follow her mom back to her pew.

I fold my hands before me and look at my arms reaching out from the puffy sleeves of my beautiful dress. After the closing prayer we walk out of the church to take pictures. The lace hem on my new lavender dress tickles my legs and I feel so very grown-up.

SURVIVING EASTER MASS

Easter is the longest mass of the year because I have to wear a dress and my feet hurt because my shoes are so stiff. The church is crowded, and hot and smelly from the incense the altar boys pour all over. Palm Sunday mass is actually longer, but Easter feels longer because chocolate eggs wait in baskets at home. There will be an Easter egg hunt, and then ham and scalloped potatoes for dinner.

I watch the families come in and count the number of girls wearing Easter bonnets. Mom never lets me get one but this year I really wanted one to go with my First Communion dress. After the procession I gaze up at the Stations of the Cross: Jesus is condemned to death, Jesus falls the first time, Jesus falls the second and third times, until eventually Jesus dies on the cross. I stand, sing, sit, kneel and half-listen as the priest talks about spring and life and death. Spring is supposed to be about life, but ever since Greg Bob died over spring break this time of year always reminds me of death. I try to stay awake and remember this is a joyful occasion even though I don't understand how Jesus rose from the dead. Why would it take three days and what was Jesus doing in that cave all that time?

Everyone takes Communion or gets a blessing, and I recount the Easter bonnets to make sure I didn't miss any. After Communion, I think about chocolate, Easter eggs and ham. Just a few more prayers, "Peace be with you" and finally it's the recessional. The altar boys, the priest, the first and second rows file out and I follow them into a cool spring morning of chocolate bunnies and marshmallow Peeps.

MISSION ABORTED

After the nine o'clock mass I follow the congregation toward the back of the church, past the confessionals and stained-glass windows. My stomach grumbles as we reach the doors at the exit and I hope Dad will let us stop for doughnuts on the way home. The tall, wooden doors are propped open and the bright sunlight hurts my eyes.

There's a table set up at the top of the steps and I hope it's cookies or hot cocoa, but instead I see models of little babies before they're born.

"Look, Mom."

"Yes, Nori, I see," but Mom hardly stops and she seems angry with the women holding the pamphlets and talking to people about the babies in their different stages. Mom doesn't look at them or smile and instead of talking to her church friends, she walks straight to the car.

I look at the little models. They remind me of the tadpoles in Mr. Jensen's pond in the spring. Each model is a little bigger with a bloody sack around it. They don't look like real babies though. Their heads and eyes are big, like aliens. It seems strange to have this set up outside church and I wonder if they're selling something. Mom gets upset when people try to sell us stuff. Mom is still mad when we get to the car so there's no way I'm asking if we can stop for doughnuts.

TALENT

We're doing a talent show at school and I'm dancing with a cane to *Putting on the Ritz*. Mitch is in the talent show too. He doesn't usually speak in public because of his accent. This will be his big debut. He's doing a commercial for Vlasic pickles. After he crunches into the pickle he says, "That's the best darn pickle I've ever heard."

I help him practice his line over and over and every time we see the commercial we try to remember exactly how the guy says it.

On the day of the talent show, I help set up folding chairs across the gym floor and the place gets packed. I do my dance and sit in the audience to watch the rest of the show. I'd been nervous for my performance, but I'm even more anxious to see if Mitch will pull off his line.

The boy doing the commercial with Mitch hands him a pickle and holds the microphone to his mouth. Mitch takes a huge bite, trying to make the pickle sound as loud as he can, but I don't think anyone notices the crack of the pickle because Mitch looks like he just ate a lemon. At home we practiced on sweet pickles, not dill, and Mitch looks like he might spit the pickle out but instead he says, "That's the best is darn pickle he ever heard" with his Korean accent. The whole audience laughs and Mitch's sour pickle commercial is the highlight of the talent show.

TREE HOUSE

Today finally feels like spring. The crabapple tree in the front yard has blossomed white and petals cover the grass like sweet-smelling snow. It's a good day to be high in the branches of a tree so I head over to the weeping willow. It's still hard for me to reach the sticks nailed to the trunk, so I have to be brave. I've done it before but I usually get a boost from Chet or Mitch. This past winter I held on in gloves, and I've grown since then so I'm sure I can do it.

I balance the toes of my shoes on the first rung and scrape against the bark with my jean-covered knees. I hug my body close to the trunk and reach as high as I can to the third rung. I don't look down. I reach with my left hand and pull my left leg up, feeling for the next rung with my tennis shoe. I think I have it, and then I don't. I slip and I'm falling. For an instant there is only sunlight shining through the limbs of the willow tree. I land on my back with a thud and can't breathe. I wonder if I've died and wait for my life to flash before my eyes. I struggle to breathe but the air won't come. My eyes tear and the blue sky above turns blurry. A car drives down the street while I lie in the backyard dying.

Then the air comes, shuddering back into my lungs, and a bird calls out from a distant tree. I look back up at the fourth rung nailed to the tree and roll over to see the root where I landed. I push myself up to my feet and walk to the house to tell Mom.

"Oh, you got the air knocked out of you." Mom dries her hands on her apron and reaches out to hug me. "That must have been scary." I lean my head into her chest and nod, trying to forget the sense of falling.

INSOMNIA

We're switching rooms. Mom and Dad say Mitch and I are getting too old to share a room because he's a boy and I'm a girl. We move beds, trade desks and slide dressers across thick carpet. Chet and Mitch share a room now. Laura has her own room and I am in Laura's old room.

I thought I'd love Laura's old room with its yellow gingham wallpaper and the built-in-bed tucked under the eave, but once I close the bedroom door I notice there are no windows. I'm trapped with all of that stale air and can't breathe. Ghosts crawl up from the basement to sleep in the closet. Nightmares seep through the cracks around the closet door. I can't fall asleep. My mind races and I can't slow it down even when I think about traveling into the emptiness of a black hole. The room gets too hot so I move to the living room to sleep on the couch so Mom will hear me if I wake up screaming.

Mom finds me sleeping in the living room every morning for two weeks straight. I tell her I can't sleep in that room. Laura never had any problems though, so we trade rooms back.

I shove my bed against the window where I can look out at Jones Road, the pine trees, and a sky full of stars at night. There are no more ghosts, no more nightmares and no more insomnia.

PEACE AND JUSTICE CAMP

Dad drives down a winding mountain road to family camp where we will stay for a week. The forest here is different, lush and green, unlike the dry, dusty forests near Bend. I look out the window from the front seat between Mom and Dad. In the backseat Laura's asleep, Chet looks silently out the window, and Mitch plays with a Rubik's cube.

I've been excited about family camp since Mom and Dad told us about it a couple months ago. There will be other families and our family will spend lots of time together. Mitch is excited too because he'll have Joe Butler to play with, but Chet and Laura didn't want to come. Laura wants to spend the summer with her friends and Chet should be playing baseball.

Dad pulls the car up to a lodge where a woman in a pink tank top and Birkenstocks like Mom's assigns us a cabin. We walk inside and Mom isn't happy. Everything looks fine to me but Mom says, "It's filthy. There aren't any mattresses. How can they expect us to sleep like this?"

It's going to be a long week.

The days are great except for the food, which I think is fine, but Mom doesn't. We meet the McGinnis family. Mr. and Mrs. McGinnis are the ones in charge of the camp and they have three adopted kids: Michael, David and Theresa. Theresa is the first black person I've met. We're close to the same age so we play when the adults have meetings. She seems just like other girls I know. She's not different even though she looks different.

While the adults are in meetings, we learn about life for kids in other countries and how we can help them. Some kids become guerillas, guerillas like soldiers, not animals. They carry guns and everything. We stage our first protest against nuclear arms testing and walk through the main lodge carrying signs we make ourselves.

There are slugs all over the camp. Chet and Michael take salt and watch them shrivel up. I watch until one of the dads catches us and says, "That's not what this camp is all about."

At dusk, Laura, Theresa and I walk to the meadow by the McGinnis' cabin. Sometimes we sneak up on deer there, or rabbits, and Laura brings her camera.

Mitch plays with Joe Butler and David McGinnis while I'm mostly bored except on afternoons when we go swimming at the river.

Nights at family camp are bad. It rains and Mom's arthritis flares up. She sleeps in the car and by the last day of camp we're all ready to go home. We wave goodbye to the other families, and Mom and Dad make plans for the McGinnis' to come visit after their last session of camp. The McGinnis family lives in St. Louis, Missouri. They aren't used to seeing animals in the wild, or slugs, and they think Oregon is beautiful.

A few weeks after camp the McGinnis' van pulls up to our house. We have water fights in the backyard and play kick-the-can in the dark. When they leave for St. Louis I wish I could go with them. I wish I could know about life in the city. What would it be like to meet someone who didn't know me as the littlest Nakada, as Chet and Laura and Mitch's little sister? I imagine taking a city bus instead of riding in a car and seeing people from different places instead of being the only one who is different all of the time. It would be like the world I see on *Sesame Street* with kids of different races saying letters and words, sometimes even in Spanish. That's a world I want to know.

FOOTBRIDGE

The house is cool even though it's a sunny August morning. Mom keeps the drapes closed to trap the cold inside and at night she throws everything open to let the cool air in again.

I'm still in bed listening to doors opening and slamming shut, and feet stomping up and down the stairs. Chet leaves for baseball practice, and Laura to volleyball. I decide to get up and make my way to the TV room. The summer sun beats down on the roof. The minutes crawl by in thirty-minute installations of *The Brady Bunch* and *The Munsters* as the temperature in the house rises.

I hear the hum of the lawn mower and smell dry grass. Chet must be back from baseball. Mitch changes the channel to *The Partridge Family*. The mower stops halfway through *Green Acres* and just as *Leave It to Beaver* starts, Chet walks in, his hair wet from showering.

"Turn it to the game."

"No," I say.

"You've been sitting in here all day. Why don't you go do something?"

"No way. It's too hot," Mitch whines.

Chet wrestles the remote from me. The Braves and Cards, third inning, Braves up 4-2.

I don't want to watch the game so I walk out to the backyard. The light shocks my eyes and I squint into the heat of the afternoon. Freshly cut grass crunches beneath my bare feet as I pass the shade of the willow tree and hop over the irrigation ditch. I plop down on the little white footbridge, my favorite summer spot, and dip my feet into the cool stream. Water tickles my toes and I imagine where else this water has been, if it was once snow I skied on this past winter, or rain that slid across the windshield of the station wagon. Maybe washed up on a beach in California and someday it will end up in a river or lake where I'll see it again.

Water skippers glide across the surface and the smell of mint rises from the bank. Mint smells like gum, but I remember from chewing it once that it doesn't taste like gum. A bright green leaf drifts downstream and gets caught in the current where the water drops a few inches. The leaf makes a circle in the water beneath my feet, comes to the surface, and gets pushed under again. I watch it rise up, and fall back through the water again and again.

I imagine I'm that leaf, drifting in a current, lazily floating along, falling and rising, knowing I'll always come to the surface. The summer sun pounds down on my dark hair as the leaf circles through the water. My toes dangle above the leaf until it escapes and floats away. I watch it disappear and long after losing sight of it, I think, I want to be that leaf.

PART THREE

MOVIE NIGHT

It's late, way past our bedtime, but we rented a VCR and the Butlers are over so Mom lets us stay up. Mom picked out some old movie for us to watch.

"Are there kids in it?" I ask.

"The little girl tells the whole story, Nori." Mom says. "You'll like it."

I take the stairs two at a time to the family room but still don't believe the movie will be any good. It's in black and white.

The family room is still warm from the hot summer day. The door to the deck is open and a chorus of crickets filters in from the night. The grown-ups just finished watching a movie about some lawyer. Mr. Butler's a lawyer too with an office downtown by St. Francis. When he gives us a ride to school in the mornings, he gives us a word and we're supposed to look it up in the dictionary and tell him what it means the next day. One day I look up culpable which means deserving punishment.

I lay on the floor as Mom turns the lights out and presses play. The tape clicks and the music starts. There is a box with crayons and a pocketknife. A marble rolls; an old watch ticks. A girl draws a bird and laughs. The people in the room fade away and my world becomes black and white. A little girl named Scout counts and swings from a tire tied to a tree branch. I follow her adventures until I can feel the thin denim of her overalls and the summer heat on her back. I imagine what Scout thinks as she sits on Atticus' lap on the porch and he tells her you never really know a man until you walk a day in his shoes. I wonder if Jem, Scout and Dill will ever get Boo Radley to come out and if Atticus will help Tom Robinson. In the end, Atticus doesn't win, Boo Radley comes out, and I think I know why it's a sin to kill a mockingbird.

The next day I pull on an old faded t-shirt and shorts fraying at the edges but I wish they were Scout's overalls. I climb up the crooked rungs on the willow tree and sit in our tree house. I look across the backyard at our neighborhood and wonder who in this town might be the Ewells or the Robinsons. I try to figure out how to get everyone to start calling me Scout but the name doesn't stick. No one calls me Scout, and the summer turns to fall.

School starts, fourth grade, and at our first recess I notice an old house on the border of the playground. I peer into its dirty windows, past the dusty green jars cluttering the sills. It's dark inside and I imagine Boo Radley in there, plotting to murder his family. I tell my classmates about it and they say I'm crazy. I think about beating them up. That's what Scout would've done, but Atticus wouldn't have liked that. Then I see Matt Rose looking in the window of the Boo Radley house and I know he's wondering.

Winter brings snow and during a close game of kickball, Richard Eigeren sends the ball flying over the fence into the Boo Radley yard.

"Go get it, Richard," Matt Rose yells.

"No way, that place is haunted."

"Oh, don't listen to Nori. She just made that up from some old movie she saw."

I look at my classmates and back to the dark house across the fence. "I'll go get it, you big babies."

I sprint out the playground gate and up the sidewalk. The red rubber ball is far into the yard, resting on a pile of dirty snow. I look at the ball and remember the time Jem pushed Scout in the tire and she landed right on the Radley porch. I take a deep breath and push open the gate. One, two, three, four, five, six, I count my steps and heartbeats like Scout did when she was waiting for Jem to get his overalls from the Radley yard. I snatch the ball and huck it over the fence where the boys dodge it, not wanting to touch the rubber contaminated by the haunted yard. A dog barks and I nearly slip on the icy walk as I slam the gate and sprint back to the safety of the schoolyard, far from Maycomb, Scout and Boo Radley.

BARBIES AND CABBAGE PATCH KIDS

Most girls get Barbies on their birthdays but Mom is funny about toys. She let Laura have an EZ Bake Oven and a play kitchen when she was little and I have dolls to dress and play with in the bathtub. Chet and Mitch have boxes full of Legos and Lincoln Logs and Mom lets us ride trikes and bikes. But on trips to the store, in the toy section, there are certain toys we can never convince her to buy. Pink Barbie boxes wait for girls and army green GI Joe boxes wait for boys, but Mom has rules. No Barbies and no guns. "It isn't a good example. Real women don't look like Barbie and guns aren't toys. They kill people."

When we go to our friends' houses the boys have action figures and toy guns and the girls have Barbies with pink convertibles and dozens of outfits. When I go over to Loretta's or Faith's we play Barbies, but they always keep the good Barbies to themselves, the ones with new leather jackets and smooth hair. I get stuck with old Barbies with dirty faces, ripped outfits and hair that's been cut in jagged chunks by kiddie scissors.

Mitch wants a gun so bad that when Chad Davidson comes over to play they use tree branches and simulate the sound effects of automatic machine gun fire. Mom snaps those sticks right in half when she catches them.

Mom has to get something at the drugstore, and Mitch and I get dragged along. I find my way to the toy aisle and don't even bother looking at the Barbie Dolls. Today I'm looking for the Cabbage Patch Kids. All the fourth grade girls have them. Nicole Wesley got one for her tenth birthday and so did Karen Thornton. They brought them to school with their little birth certificates. I walk toward a towering display of olive green Cabbage Patch Kid boxes and peer through the cellophane. There are dolls like Nicole's and

Karen's and then I see the one I want. She has straight brown hair and brown eyes like mine.

I call Mom and she stands with me looking at the Cabbage Patch Kids. "Oh, Nori, those dolls cost over fifty dollars."

I look up at her and hope the tears welling up in my eyes will make her reconsider.

She doesn't.

I stare at a doll with blonde curly hair and green eyes and accept that I will be left out of this toy too. When Karen and Nicole and Carrie bring their Cabbage Patch Kids and play with them at recess next to the handball courts, I'll play dodge ball instead.

RICE

Standing on a chair at the kitchen sink I measure out four cups of rice and watch the tiny grains fall like hail into the metal rice bowl. I turn the faucet on and let the cold water run. My hands nearly freeze as I drag my fingers through the cold water and across the hard grains of rice.

Mom stands at the counter behind me, her knife piercing through the ligament and bone of a chicken.

"How clear should it get?" I ask, studying the cloudy water.

"Just rinse it three or four times."

I tilt the metal bowl and let the water flow out. I've watched Mom wash rice so many times I've memorized the angle that keeps the grains from falling out. After two or three rinses, I fill the bowl until the water reaches the first line in my finger. I plug in the rice cooker, place the bowl inside and press COOK.

Auntie Grace gave Mom the rice cooker when she married Dad. Mom says it's her favorite wedding gift because we use it every day. I thought everyone ate rice until first grade when Ms. Bartell asked what people ate for Thanksgiving and I added rice to the list of turkey, cranberries and pumpkin pie. No one else ate rice for Thanksgiving and I said they were all missing out.

The smell of rice cooking fills the kitchen and puffs of steam fog up the windows. Mom fries the chicken and makes gravy. I rinse lettuce for a salad and as I tear the thin leaves I hear the rice cooker pop. We sit down to dinner and the six of us hold hands for grace. *Bless us, oh Lord, for these Thy gifts which we are about to receive, from Thy bounty, through Christ, our Lord, Amen.* We've gotten it down to record speed: two and a half seconds.

Mom plates pieces of chicken, salad and rice. I pour the thick gravy over the rice I measured and washed. I mix the gravy and rice and when I take my first bite it's perfect.

MALLARDS

A family of mallard ducks lives in the irrigation ditches of our neighborhood. I can follow the seasons by watching them come and go. Spring is here when the brown, speckled mother and her green-headed companion show up. Their mating scares me (all beaks and feathers) but Mom assures me this is the way ducks do it. When the ducklings arrive they are tiny yellow cotton balls of high chirps. They follow after their mother in a trail across our lawn. I wish the city would put up a duck crossing sign on our street because I worry that the cars speeding down Jones Road will squish those little ducklings.

The ducks spend the summer and fall growing up and we know winter is on its way when they disappear. This year a couple of the ducks think they can stick it out for the winter. I wonder what will happen to those silly ducks that refuse to fly south.

After the first cold spell, the irrigation ditches run dry leaving a crust of ice where the water used to flow. Mitch, Chet and I walk through the dried up ditch, breaking up chunks of ice with each step. Chet spots a big, icy something and pokes at it with a stick. He turns it on its side. It's one of our ducks, frozen solid.

"We should bury it," I say, feeling sorry for the poor duck, too stubborn to fly south.

"No way," Chet scoffs. "The ground is too hard. We'll have to come back in the spring." He drops the stick and we leave that frozen duck at the bottom of the dry ditch to be buried in snow.

SNOW DAY

I wake up and it's still dark outside. I don't need to look out the window to know it snowed last night. From my cocoon of warm blankets, I hear a car pass by the house. Cars sound totally different driving down roads covered in snow. They move in near silence or with the hum of chains on their tires. My alarm goes off and I reach into the cold room to turn it off. I don't want to get up. Maybe enough snow fell to cancel school. The excitement of this possibility wakes me up completely.

I hold my breath and jump from the warmth of bed into the cold of my bedroom. I sprint downstairs to stand by the woodstove in the living room. Mom makes breakfast in the kitchen and outside snow continues to fall. It was snowing last night when I went to bed and it still hasn't stopped. A clean white blanket covers the grass and the houses wear a thick layer of marshmallow fluff. Tree branches droop with the snow's weight making them look old and weary. From a glance at the fence posts it looks like at least eight inches have fallen.

Mom carries a teakettle into the living room. She sets it on top of the woodstove and several water droplets dance on the iron top before hissing into steam. "No school today, Nori. Snow day."

"Yes," I say and smile.

Mom heads back into the kitchen to finish making breakfast like she does every morning. I stand facing the woodstove until the fronts of my pajamas are so hot I'm afraid they might catch on fire. I get as close as I can without touching, but the scars on my kneecaps mark the times I've inched too close and singed the skin off. I turn around and warm my back as snowflakes dance through the crabapple tree's icy branches. Cars drive by every so often while the snow falls, falls, falls.

Mitch comes downstairs when breakfast is ready. Mom makes German oven pancakes: hot, fluffy, and buttery with a sweet dusting of powered sugar. Chet and Laura are still asleep, but Mitch and I can hardly wait to get out into all that snow.

We bundle up in our ski clothes: gloves, hats and warm-ups. It's so quiet outside that our voices seem to carry forever but we barely talk as we shovel the driveway. Our house sits just below the road so even the littlest bit of snow makes it tough to back the car out and if we don't shovel it, we'll find ourselves snowed in. At first it's fun scooping shovelfuls of perfect, clean snow. We start at the bottom and work our way up. But by the time we make it to the top, another inch has fallen along the bottom. We're too cold and tired to play in the snow so we head back inside.

It's still snowing hard when Dad gets home around 2:00. His boss closed the office so everyone could get home before dark. He says there's almost two feet out there. I've seen snow like this on the mountain, but never here in town. It reminds me of pictures from when Laura and Chet were little and there was so much snow they could step off the top of the jungle gym, fall into the deep snow and not hit the ground.

That night, I turn on the lights that shine on the basketball court to see if it's still snowing. Tiny white flakes continue to drift down and I'm pretty sure we'll get to miss another day of school.

From the warmth of my bed I dream about the roar of a snowplow clearing snow and ice from the roads. Flashing yellow lights cast spinning patterns across my bedroom walls and then, the sander comes, ruining the perfect white, silence of snow. Once the snowplow and sander come, cars will take to the streets and the heat from their tires will melt the snow. When the roads clear, the school buses will run, and we'll have to go back to school.

But this morning Jones Road remains white, icy and slick. All of Bend's snowplows can't clear two feet of snow from the main roads fast enough for school to open.

That afternoon the clouds open to brilliant blue skies. Mitch and I shovel the driveway one last time in blinding sunlight. The wind showers us with shimmering crystals blown from treetops. When the driveway is clear, we've created two enormous snow banks on the sides of our driveway. We plan for a snowball fight to end all snowball fights. We build forts on both sides of the driveway and stockpile them with snowball ammunition. When Chet comes out, we'll pummel him. This is revenge for every surprise snowball Chet has ever exploded off our heads, for every whitewash that left our faces red, raw and wet.

We work up a sweat in the freezing cold, until our wall is solid and the shelves in our wall are loaded with snowballs. Chad Davidson, and Joe and Becky Butler come over to help and when we're ready Mitch runs inside to ask Chet if he wants to have a snowball fight. Chet's been sitting inside all of this time but he finally decides to come out and join us.

Hiding behind our fortress, we watch the garage door creep open. Chet stands there in his parka and boots. We fire and snowballs fly from everywhere. Even though only a couple actually hit him, it's worth seeing him run, except he runs straight for our fort. Becky and I scream as we desert our side leaving Chet with a wall to hide behind and a never-ending snowball supply. Chet lobs snowballs perfectly so they fly over our wall and land on us. I can't believe it's only him over there as snowballs rain down on us. There's no hope in sight so I run inside to escape the massacre.

That afternoon I hear the dreaded hum and jingle of a snowplow followed by the ticking of a sander. Instantly, our perfect white world turns dirty and cinder-covered. The next morning, it's back to school and I pray for another snow day.

TIGER AND BOB THE CAT

Mitch has wanted another cat ever since Neko went away. Even though our family has terrible luck with pets we rescue Bob and Tiger from a farm near Redmond: two yellow and orange brothers. Bob the Cat is the crazy evil one. He hisses and howls if you come close to him and he sneaks everywhere he goes. His eyes dart and he looks like that cat from the Opus cartoon, Bill the Cat, who's on drugs. Tiger is the good cat. He rubs against your leg and purrs when he sits on your lap.

One morning I'm eating oatmeal at the kitchen table. I warm my hands around the ceramic bowl and look out the window. A trace of snow has fallen over night, dusting the rooftops. The sun rises over the Ochocos, chasing the stars like static from the sky. I spot Tiger walking on tiny cat feet across the frozen backyard.

Laura walks in and glares at the pot of oatmeal Mom left on the stove. She dumps some in her bowl and sits down at the table. We say nothing. I don't even know who my sister is before 10:30 am. She is another creature, angry and sullen.

Mitch comes in. "Good morning girls. Mmm. Oatmeal. Perfect for a cold morning."

I look back at my bowl not sure which of my siblings is worse company first thing in the morning. Two more bites.

Outside, Tiger tiptoes across the snow on tender feet and then paws at something buried in the snow. I can tell by the dirty, orange fur that it's Bob the Cat. He doesn't move. He's a frozen, snow-covered lump like that stubborn duck still buried in the ditch.

Mitch and I look out the window with horror, but Laura takes another bite of oatmeal and says, "Well, Mitch, looks like your cat froze to death last night."

Mitch runs outside to Bob the Cat as I watch from the table, trying to keep the oatmeal from climbing its way back up.

ME V. BOYS

In fourth grade, I'm suddenly not supposed to be better than the boys at sports anymore. I don't care though. I still play dodgeball and get everyone out except Richard Eguiren and Matt Rose. Our teacher, Mrs. Reynolds, had a tumor in her leg last year and she walks with a cane now. If your desk is messy, she'll tip it over and all your stuff will fall on the floor.

She reads us *James and the Giant Peach*. I love the line drawings of James' mean aunts and the birds carrying the enormous peach high into the sky. My favorite part is when the cloud people attack the peach and hurl handfuls of cloud like snowballs. Even though I've never been in an airplane, I bet that's what it's like to be close to the sun with a layer of clouds beneath you.

That Halloween, all of the boys dress up like ninjas. That's when Matt Rose starts calling me Ninja Nori even though I dress up like the Easter Bunny. All of the boys think the name Ninja Nori is funny and I guess it's better than being called a geisha girl. That's what Matt called me in the third grade. One day Matt sees some seaweed at the grocery store, but the package doesn't say seaweed, it says *nori*, so now, instead of being Ninja Nori, I'm Seaweed.

I tell Mom about it and she says to just ignore those boys. She says maybe they like me and that's why they tease me so much. I don't know about that. I think boys are gross and mean except for Daniel Callahan who is still the cutest. Maybe if he teased me more I'd like it, but he just ignores me.

Some of the fifth and sixth graders are going out and maybe when I'm in the fifth or sixth grade, if it's the right boy, I won't think it's so gross anymore.

STREP THROAT

I open my eyes in the half-light and it takes me a minute to recognize the living room. It's not morning or night and it's so quiet that all I hear is my breathing and the rustle of blankets against my sweaty skin. My pajamas stick to my legs and back, but my skin feels cold and goose bumps cover my body like tiny grains of sand.

Dr. Hakala says I have strep throat so I can't go to school until Thursday. Today is my tenth birthday. It's the worst birthday ever.

Chet, Laura and Mitch are at school. Dad's at work, and Mom is at the store picking up some soup, crackers, and soda pop. That's what we eat on sick days.

Mom comes home and I drink the 7up because it's the only time we ever get soda, but it hurts to swallow, and the bubbles make it worse.

We cancel my birthday party.

I watch shows from when I was little: *Sesame Street* and *Captain Kangaroo*. I wonder what all the kids at school are doing. I watch old reruns of *MASH* and *The Barney Miller Show* until I fall asleep.

Mitch and Laura come home from school. Chet is at baseball practice.

"After dinner we'll open your presents," Mom yells to me from the kitchen.

"I'm not hungry."

"Fine, then. Open them now."

There's a pile of gifts on the dining room table. We usually don't get much for our birthday, but Mom feels bad because I'm sick. I rip into the bright yellow and orange wrapping paper. A sticker book! Stickers! Stationary! Markers! Looking at all of my favorite things, I forget how awful my birthday has been. I want to save the stickers, especially the scratch and sniff ones, and try not to scratch them too much or the color and smell will fade away.

Dad comes home from work and Chet from baseball. Everyone eats dinner but I stay in the living room looking at my stickers and flipping through the toy section of the Sears catalog. When they finish eating, I show Mitch what I like.

"Nori," Mom says from behind the newspaper. "You got all these nice presents and instead of enjoying them you're looking at more things you want."

I glance back at the catalog and feel like a selfish brat. I think of the book *The Perfect Pancake* with the woman who makes perfect pancakes and everyone says they are the best until a man comes to town and tells the woman they are just okay. The woman keeps making pancakes for the man and he is so greedy he gets sick on all those pancakes.

"Sorry, Mom," I say, placing the catalog back on the shelf. "Thanks for everything."

Mom keeps reading the paper. I look at my stickers, markers and stationary and it all seems pretty perfect. I try to swallow, but it still hurts.

SUMMER

Every summer we're on swim team. Mitch and I ride our bikes to the pool like Chet and Laura used to. The water in the outdoor pool at the Juniper Aquatic Center is clear and cool. I push off the wall like an arrow and start my 200 free. I breathe in and out and try to keep my kick steady. I can't wait for the 200 breast we have coming up. It's my best stroke.

I cut through the water and remember when I was little and could hardly make it the length of the indoor pool. I had to make myself not hold on to the lane lines, but that was a long time ago. It's still hard now with the long workouts, but I know I can make it. It's just a matter of timing: breathe, kick, stroke, breathe, kick, stroke.

It's too hot and I'm bored. I walk out to the big freezer in the garage and open the door to a blast of cold air. I pull a half-empty Popsicle bag from beneath the frozen ground beef. Why are the grape ones always gone by the time I get here? No more cherry either. Just orange. I take one and shut the freezer door. I open the top of the wrapper, take a deep breath and blow the thin plastic so it puffs out like a transparent puffer fish that just ate an orange Popsicle. I pull the plastic off before it gets stuck and gooey.

I hit the button to the garage door opener and as the door lifts the sun shocks my eyes. I sit on the rock wall by the driveway in the pounding sun and the hot lava rock edges dig into my legs.

The day doesn't feel so hot now that I'm eating a Popsicle. I have to eat it fast though. It melts and drips, making my fingers sticky. I lean over so it drips onto the ground. A bunch of ants scurry away from the falling drops. My Popsicle melts in orange globs drowning ants in sugar-water.

After church today we're going to Scout Lake. Mom packs lunch in the heavy red cooler and Dad loads it into the car. We put on our swimsuits, grab beach towels and pack the inflatable raft.

Dad drives out Highway 97, past the Bend River Mall and toward Sisters. On that part of the highway you can see the whole mountain range and Black Butte rising in the distance. On really clear days you can see Mt. Hood, Mt. Washington and Mt. St. Helens. We drive through Sisters with its old western storefronts, past Black Butte Ranch and down a narrow road to Scout Lake.

Scout Lake is not very big. If we really wanted to we could probably swim across and back. The lake is shallow so the water stays warm but Chet says it's because so many people pee in it. We set up a campsite and splash around in the water trying not to touch the bottom because the soft mud feels gross on our bare feet.

There's a rope swing and once in a while someone splashes into the lake. Mitch and I hike to where the rope is tied to a tree. The rope has several knots where you can hold on with your hands and feet. We watch a teenager swing out crooked and almost hit one of the trees.

When we hike back Dad says he'll take us over to the rope swing even though Mom doesn't want him to. Chet and Laura say they're going to go, but Mitch and I aren't sure. The five of us walk along the shore as a boy clings to the rope, swings through the thin air and drops into the lake. With each swing I hold my breath until a head bobs up in the water. Another survivor.

We reach the tree and climb over its thick roots to the take-off. Chet climbs up and balances on the branch as the rope swings to his hands. He misses it the first time and someone has to swim out and throw it back in. Chet catches the rope and quickly, without thinking, he pushes off the tree and swings out into the middle of the lake where he drops with a perfect splash. The rope swings back and Dad catches it. "Who's next?"

Laura walks toward the tree. She climbs, balances and waits a little longer than Chet did. She listens to Dad remind her to push off straight so she doesn't hit any of the trees. He tells her to wait for the rope to swing out far enough that she doesn't hurt herself dropping into shallow water. Laura's arms shake but she pushes off and then drops into deep dark-blue water.

Mitch is smaller than Chet and Laura and when he grabs the very end of the rope Dad tells him he'll have to climb up so his feet won't drag. Mitch lets go of the tree, scurries up the rope as it swings through the air and then splashes into lake. He floats to the surface, emerging with one of his biggest smiles ever.

It's my turn. I walk up the slippery path to the take-off branch. Dad swings the rope to me and I barely grab it. I try to reach the lowest knot on the rope. "I can't get it, Dad."

"It's okay. You'll just have to climb up like Mitch did and make sure you push off straight."

If Mitch can do it, I can do it. I grip the thick, wet end of the rope with the fingertips of my left hand and hold the tree's rough trunk with my right arm. What if I don't push off right and slam into one of those trees, or don't climb up high enough or drop in water that's too shallow? I could die. I try not to think about it.

"Come on, Nori!" Chet yells from the water.

"Just hold on tight and then let go," Laura tells me.

"You can do it, Nor!" Mitch adds.

My siblings tread water waiting for me to join them.

"You don't have to do this," Dad says and I look up to where the rope is tied to the tree, a long pendulum.

"I can." My voice shakes. I take a deep breath and imagine exactly what I need to do: let go, push off, reach up, pull my feet up and then reach up to the next knot and the next.

"Once you go, you have to go. You can't stop in the middle, so decide now." Dad is getting impatient.

Ready, set, go. I push off, grab the first knot and climb. The wind rushes through my hair as I pull myself up, up, up the rope. I look down and I'm over the water. Wait, I tell myself, wait, and just as the rope pauses in midair I let go and plunge into the lake. The cool water swallows me and my feet don't touch the bottom. I kick to the surface. My heart beats fast and all I want to do is try it again.

The four of us bob up and down in the warm water of the lake, and then swim together toward the shore. Chet's strong freestyle pulls him ahead of us and Mitch follows. Laura and I take our time, kicking and gliding toward the water's edge where Dad waits for us to walk back and eat lunch with Mom.

RATED R

Sue Butler is over and Mom rented a VCR and movies. We're watching *Flashdance*. It's rated R. I've never seen a rated R movie at our house before. I sit close to the TV in the lime green armchair and watch. The music is fast and I like it. I think I understand what is happening with the woman gliding and jumping, working and trying hard. There is cussing and kissing and I feel grown-up watching this movie that's not about kids or for kids.

Then, comes the sexy part and I feel something new, something warm and sugary that I've never felt before. I look at Mom but she isn't looking at me. She stares at the screen and I wonder if she's feeling it, or if Sue Butler is. I guess you aren't supposed to talk about it and I feel too young to be watching this. Part of me wants to cover my eyes but that's such a little kid thing to do and I told Mom I could handle watching this. Besides, the feeling isn't bad. It's really kind of nice so I keep watching.

I can't imagine ever doing anything like what that man and woman do and I don't even like to think of Mom and Dad doing that, but I know they must. They used to let me climb into bed with them but now it's off limits. Maybe that's why they don't want any of us in their bedroom. Maybe their bedroom is rated R.

THE COSBYS

The Cosby Show starts with Bill Cosby dancing with his wife and each of his kids. It's one of the only shows Mom likes to watch with us. I like the Cosbys better than the Keetons who are on right after them. I used to like the Bradys but the Cosbys are better than any other TV family even though they're nothing like our family. Their family is rich and they live in the city, but Theo reminds me of Chet sometimes and I think I'm like Rudy. I guess it's just nice to see a family that's different, that isn't *The Brady Bunch* or *The Partridge Family*. I wonder why there aren't any Asian families on TV or families with adopted kids. Well, there's *Diff'rent Strokes*, but that doesn't feel like a real family. I try to imagine a show with a Japanese family or a mixed race family, but I don't think they have shows like that on TV. There don't seem to be any families like ours out there.

ALTAR GIRL

I wait for mass to start for like the millionth Sunday. Today we're early because Mitch is serving as an altar boy. I watch the front of the church and wait for him to light the candles. He walks out from behind a red curtain and I wonder what's back there. He wears a long red robe with a white apron on top. A long gold pole with a flame at the tip extends his reach and once the candles are all lit, he disappears behind the curtain again.

We stand for the procession and here comes Mitch with two other altar boys, Jimmy Olson and Mark Smith. Mitch and Mark carry candles while Jimmy carries a cross. The priest walks behind the boys with his palms pressed together in front of him.

All through mass, I watch Mitch instead of the priest, or the choir, or the readers. I want to make him laugh while he's up there, stick my tongue out or something, but when I barely even smile Mom looks at me like I'm sin. After mass I ask Mom if I can be an altar boy.

"I don't know. There have never been any girl altar boys, but I'll ask Father Kelly."

A few days later, even though I've forgotten all about being an altar boy, Mom calls me down from my room. "I talked to Father Kelly and he can't let you be an altar boy, but he said you can write and ask the Cardinal."

Dear Cardinal O'Connell-

I go to church at St. Francis in Bend. I am in the fifth grade at St. Francis Elementary and I've done my First Confession and my First Communion. Both of my brothers were altar boys and I think I could be an altar boy even though I am a girl. I could light the candles, ring the bells, and listen to the priest. I would do just as good as any of the boys and would like your permission.

Thank you, Nori Nakada

After a few weeks, when I get home from school a creamy white envelope waits for me on the dining room table.

Dear Nori,

Thank you for your commitment to the Church and Our Lord, Jesus Christ. Being an altar boy is the holiest way for our young men to serve. The altar boy witnesses the blessing of the Holy Sacrament as we remember Our Lord's Last Supper. Just as men served Jesus on Good Friday, every mass provides the altar boy with an opportunity to see if he is called to serve as a priest. A girl cannot assist in this Holy Sacrament as no women attended The Last Supper and girls cannot receive this most holy calling. There are many other ways for you to serve our church community such as singing in the children's choir or helping with the collection. This is the way of The Lord.

Peace and Blessings, Cardinal O'Connell

My heart drops a little as I study the fancy typing on the thick paper. I hand the letter to Mom. I watch her face, which is always a little red even when she wears make up, but as she reads and then rereads the letter, her cheeks look hot and I can tell she's mad. She hands the letter to me and after a deep breath she puts her arm around my shoulders.

I watch Mitch the next Sunday, and when he looks at me I try to make him laugh. I stick out my tongue and roll my eyes and put my hands over my ears when Mom sings the hymns. He grins at me and then looks away. He doesn't look at me again for the rest of the mass.

Mitch doesn't last long as an altar boy. He tells me church is just as boring when you're an altar boy. I trust him, but I'll never know.

PRAYING FOR BETHY

It's Monday morning; time for the school prayer. All of the students sit in the dark hallway as the principal, Sister Marian, lights a candle. We pray for Mrs. Reynolds' cancer to stay in remission and for the Robinsons whose Mom was in a car accident. Today there is a new person to pray for, Bethy Hurley. She's in the fourth grade and she's being treated for leukemia. Sister Marian prays for Bethy, her sisters, her parents and for the doctors treating her. We bow our heads.

Our Father, who art in Heaven, hallowed be Thy name, Thy kingdom come, Thy will be done on earth as it is in Heaven. Give us this day our daily bread, and forgive us our trespasses as we forgive those who trespass against us. And lead us not into temptation but deliver us from evil. Amen.

Whispers rise from the dark and I think about Bethy Hurley. I remember the times we played at her house and when we drove to Eugene for the Hershey Track Meet with our big sisters. It's hard to imagine that she is so sick we are praying for her. You have to be really sick, not like a cold, or the flu. If the school prays for you, you might die.

I'm standing with the children's choir at church the next Sunday when the Hurley family comes in. Bethy walks down the aisle, but she looks different. She slides down the pew next to her older sisters Mary and Katherine, and her younger sister Anne. The Hurley family always looks so perfect in their Sunday dresses with their hair all done. I've always liked their mom, too. She smiles and is nice to everyone even though her daughter is sick.

I smile and wave to Bethy when we stand up to sing for the procession. I try not to stare at her, but I want to figure out what has changed. Her hair doesn't look long and curly like it used to and her skin looks thin like tissue paper wet with glue. Even though she's always been small, she looks even tinier.

After mass I ask Mom what was wrong with Bethy's hair and she tells me the radiation therapy makes your hair fall out so she has to wear a wig. I'd always thought wigs were for old ladies, not little girls and I hate thinking of Bethy taking her hair off before she goes to bed at night.

That night I pray for Bethy Hurley. I usually feel weird praying, like I'm begging God for things, but this time it feels different. I really want Bethy to get better, and I fall asleep praying for God to help her.

Mom gets me a book called *Sadako and the Thousand Paper Cranes*. It's about a little girl with leukemia. She tries to fold a thousand paper cranes to get better. She folds and folds but Sadako dies before she gets a thousand. Our cousin Mari taught Laura and I how to fold the cranes once, but I can't remember where the creases go. I wish I could remember. Then I could fold a thousand cranes for Bethy.

FORTUNE COOKIES

We have a Betty Crocker cookbook for kids with easy recipes Laura and I can make by ourselves. Butterscotch brownies are my favorite. One year at Christmas we made Auntie Grace a birthday cake that looked like an igloo covered in sugar that sparkled like snow. Even though my sister and I play sports and don't usually do girlie things, we both like to bake.

I find a recipe for fortune cookies in a magazine. It only has four ingredients and the directions look easy so I decide to try. First, I write the fortunes. I pull out a piece of notebook paper from the clutter on Mom's desk and dig through the drawer until I find a blue ballpoint pen.

I start with easy ones. "You will have the best day of your life." I write in my neatest fifth grade printing. I try to think of fortunes I've read in the cookies at Eddie's, but I can't remember any.

I look out the window and watch Tiger walk across the basketball court. "Your cat will die tomorrow." I chuckle and imagine Mitch opening the fortune. I try to think of a terrible fortune for each of my siblings. "Your boyfriend will break up with you" is for Laura. For Chet I write, "You are a mean, mean, brother" but I cross that one out. That's not a fortune. Instead, I write "You will be nice to your littlest sister."

I cut the fortunes into strips and then make the cookie batter. I spread two discs of the gooey batter onto a cookie sheet. I look into the still-full bowl and realize these cookies are going to take forever.

After seven minutes, the cookies are done and I pull them out of the oven. I can only bake two at a time because I have to fold them while they're still hot. I slide the spatula under the warm, golden brown cookies and place one of my fortunes inside. It's a good one: "You will get a puppy." I hope Mom opens that one and thinks it's a sign from God. I fold the hot cookie in half twice and then set it in an empty egg carton to cool.

It takes me over an hour to make 24 cookies and I eat a couple of the best fortunes: "You will inherit a million dollars," and "You will have a many friends."

Mom comes into the kitchen from her nap. Her hair is flat on one side. She looks at my egg cartons full of cookies. "Those look great, Nori, like real fortune cookies."

They don't, though. They are brown around the edges, but not all the way through like real fortune cookies. After they cool I let my brothers and sister eat some. They say my cookies taste even better than regular fortune cookies and they laugh at the fortunes.

Later that afternoon, we go to Juniper Park for a church picnic. I run off to play soccer with some kids. When I come back, I see that Mom has brought the fortune cookies. I try to remember what I wrote on all of the fortunes and hope Mitch, Laura and Chet already opened the mean ones. Mom tells some women from church how her daughter made these cookies. "Isn't she creative?" Mom brags. I don't want to be there when anyone eats them so I run to the swings and forget about the fortune cookies.

When I come back Mom has packed up our things and is ready to go. "Nori," she yells when she sees me coming. "Get over here, now."

Uh oh. I bet someone like Mrs. Hensen, the orchestra teacher with a British accent, got one of the really bad fortunes. She wouldn't think any of my fortunes are funny.

"Your cat will die tomorrow?" Mom looks as if she's never seen me before.

"I didn't know you were bringing them to a church thing. I thought only our family would eat them."

"You will have bad luck for the rest of your life?" Mom quotes another fortune.

I look down at the ground and see ants swarming around the stem of a strawberry. I wonder how much trouble I'm in.

We walk back to the car, and I decide I'll never try to predict the future again. Once we start driving though, I see Mom trying not to laugh.

CHRISTMAS

Mom guides our station wagon down 8th Street toward St. Francis. Two inches of snow fell last night. The world is quiet and the sun sparkles off the Cascades in the morning light, but it didn't snow enough to cancel school. The main streets have been plowed and sanded with red cinders, but the tires occasionally slip. Mom clenches the steering wheel and I'm sure her hands are sweaty inside her black leather gloves. Mitch sits in the back seat staring out the window. He's mad at me because I overslept and he had to shovel the driveway by himself. Mitch's anger is silent and I wish he would just yell at me and get it over with, but instead he won't speak to me for days or look me in the eye.

It's the last day before Christmas break. Mitch walks toward Mr. Douglass' sixth grade classroom, and I follow him to see if Jimmy Olson is there. Jimmy is the cutest sixth grade boy and the best player on the basketball team. Mr. Douglass catches me though, so I run across the hall to my classroom.

At 8:45, we walk to the church for mass. I love the smell of the church just before Christmas. Evergreen trees surround the altar so the statues of Mary and St. Francis look like they are standing in the treetops of a forest. Four advent candles nestle inside a wreath of pine boughs and today the altar boys will light the three pink ones. The purple one will be lit on the last week of advent.

When the sixth graders come in I look for Jimmy. Matt Rose notices me turning around and rolls his eyes. If we weren't in church, he would say, "Ooh, Nori, there's your boyfriend," and I punch him in the arm. Jimmy doesn't walk in with the sixth graders, though. He must be absent.

After mass, there's recess, math, and then lunch. In Mrs. O'Rourke's room I rest my head on the cold desk and watch the clock's second hand. It sweeps around slowly until it reaches the 12 and the minute hand moves. 2:49.

I'm done with the Christmas cards Mrs. O'Rourke had us make and I watch her. She pulls a Kleenex out of the box on her desk and wipes at her nose. She looks up at the clock, and then back at the papers she's grading. What is she waiting for? I look back at the clock and watch the second hand again. I fast forward to tonight when the relatives get into town.

We will go over to the Riverside Inn. My cousins will be there along with my aunties and uncles. In the hotel's kitchenette, Auntie Jo will make spaghetti sauce and Auntie Suma will boil the noodles. Auntie Grace will prepare a salad and garlic bread. After dinner, we'll watch basketball from a brown L shaped couch and eat See's Candy. Everyone will say how grown up Mitch and I have gotten and the uncles will ask about Laura and Chet's basketball seasons. Dad will let everyone know how much snow is on the mountain and Auntie Grace will make sandwiches for tomorrow.

Christmas is church and Jesus, evergreen trees and the advent wreath, but more than anything it's Dad's family driving up from California. They bring noise, laughter and food we never eat except at Christmas: *senbei* rice crackers, sushi, teriyaki chicken, and vegetable tempura. It's the one week we're Japanese.

The minute hand is at 2:54 when Mrs. O'Rourke finally tells us to get our coats and backpacks and line up at the door.

We go to the Riverside for dinner that night, and even though we've been lighting the advent candles for weeks, Christmas is finally here when I knock on the door at the hotel and my cousin, Pam, answers. Then everything happens just like I imagined it from my desk in Mrs. O'Rourke's class.

When I wake up the next morning, it's still dark outside. We load the car and meet the rest of the family at the hotel to caravan to Mt. Bachelor. It takes forever to wind through Bend's icy streets and up Century Drive. The sky clears and the ski report says there are six new inches. Dad wants to be the first on the mountain so he can break in this new layer of powder. Maybe he'll even ski the cinder cone leaving perfect S-turns curving down the slope.

My legs tingle from the vibration of studded snow tires and Laura braids my hair to pass the time. We gain altitude and the snow banks grow tall around us making the bright blue sky seem far away. Around the final bend in the road Mt. Bachelor appears, a glacier of ice and rock pushing up into the cold. It's so huge it takes my breath away even though I see it from a distance every day.

We come to a stop near the main lodge, and I tumble out of the car into a cold that snaps at my face. I stuff my feet into stiff boots, pull on my itchy hat and stretch my goggles over the hat. My skis—once Mitch's skis, before that Laura's skis and before that Chet's—balance on my shoulder. I grab my battered poles and I'm ready.

Dad, Chet, Laura, Mitch, all my aunties, uncles, and cousins pound toward the slopes. Today I follow Dad to the black chair. He's going to ski with me this morning to see if I can keep up. This could be my year to ski with the older cousins, if they let me.

Dad clips my lift ticket to my parka and we scatter until lunch. I watch Uncle Yosh and Auntie Suma, Uncle Sat and Auntie Grace ski off and remember the days I spent with them on the orange and yellow chairs. On cold days, Auntie Grace and I used to sneak into the doughnut shop in the main lodge and watch the rings of dough floating in sizzling oil, turning golden brown. We nibbled doughnuts, sipped hot cocoa and watched the frozen slopes from the warmth of the lodge.

I wait in the lift line and watch the skiers ahead of me load onto the chair. I lean forward on my poles to stretch my legs and when it's our turn, the chair lifts me higher than I've ever been before. My legs dangle in the thin air as the chair swings. I'm sweaty under all my layers and my stomach drops. Suddenly, I'm scared like I used to be on the kiddy chair. I look up the steep hill and wonder what's up there. What if I fall and break my leg like Laura did? Maybe I'm not good enough. Dad looks over at me. "Looks like we're some of the first ones up here, Noriko. Hardly any tracks."

Far below me, two skiers make fresh turns in the pristine powder down black lift line. They turn effortlessly and float on top of the snow, weightless.

"See how that guy uses his poles? Pole, turn, pole, turn."

I watch him and see a rhythm of skiing beyond the snowplow. At the top of the lift, I slide off the chair and it isn't much different than the other lifts. I follow Dad past the beginners on the easy run to the top of Old Skyliner. The run is steep and narrow and the trees feel so close. Only a few skiers have left tracks and Dad says he'll follow me. I wonder if he thinks I'll fall and he'll have to collect my skis if I pop out of my bindings. I try to be fearless, to dive down the run and keep my poles in front of me, planting them like Dad told me. I turn and lean and a quick twenty turns later, I'm down the run.

Dad slides to a hockey stop beside me. "Looking good, Kiddo."

We make our way up and down the mountain all morning and after lunch Dad still wants to ski with me. He doesn't care that he missed the cinder cone and its knee-deep powder.

We ski Old Skyliner until the sun falls behind the mountain and the snow turns grey in its shadow. On the ride up for the last run of the day Dad fiddles with his goggles. "I think you're ready to ski with the big kids," He clears the fog from the plastic lenses. "Ready for black lift line?"

I look down at the skiers carving into the ice on the steep slope. Their edges slide and cut into the mountainside. "Really, Dad? You think I can make it?"

"Sure. You'll be fine."

I follow Dad as he leads me to the top of a run that doesn't have a sign. I look up at the chairs of the black lift swaying in the wind. The cable has stopped and the mountain is closing for the night. The steep slope waits, dark in mountain's shadow, and the moguls are higher than my waist. We balance on our edges and in the silence Dad says, "Go ahead."

"No, you go first," I tell him. "I'll see you at the bottom."

Dad drops into the run and turns gracefully, his skis perfectly parallel. He glides down the mountain and I drop in behind him, following his line, his voice echoing in my mind, "If you want to slow down, just turn."

I let my skis run and then pick out my own path through the moguls. My skis feel light, just extensions of my feet. Ice scrapes from beneath the packed powder and my legs bounce out of each turn. I feel the rhythm of the run as I float down the mountain and don't stop until I see the lights of the lodge at the bottom of the hill. Dad waits for me, smiling like he only does on skis. I stop beside him and we step out of our bindings. We walk back to the car and both of us know I can keep up.

DIVORCE

We're at church but I'm not thinking about God or Jesus. Mr. Butler is leading the choir. He holds a guitar and sings Mom's favorite song into the microphone. I wonder if hearing him sing it ruins it for her. *Morning has broken like the first morning. Blackbird has spoken, like the first bird.* When Mr. Butler sings, *Praise for the singing*, I doubt Mom praises his singing.

I can feel Mom's anger as she watches the processional. "I don't know how they can let him sing at mass," Mom whispers to Dad. "The church won't let people who divorce get remarried, but they'll let them sing in the church choir."

Mom doesn't think I can hear her, but I can. I've been listening very carefully and even though Mom doesn't want to talk about it in front of us we all know the Butlers are getting divorced. We've been friends with the Butlers forever. They watch movies at our house and ride bikes with us in the field.

Mr. Butler has a nice voice and it's hard for me to not like him. But he doesn't live with his family anymore or take us to school.

The priest says the beginning of mass and we sit down. Sue Butler, Becky, Joe and Annie sit one pew in front of us. Joe's hair is wet like he just got out of the shower. Becky looks at her hands. I wonder how they feel seeing their Dad in front of the church instead of at home.

It's time to kneel and pray. I rest my hands on the pew in front of me and remember all the times we've play with the Butler's. After Annie was born their house smelled like milk and we ran up and down the steep staircase between the attic and the living room. Then they moved next door to the Davidsons and got a trampoline that we jumped on for hours. Whenever the Butlers went out of town we watered their plants and watched their rabbits. I wish it wasn't so hard to go over to the Butlers to play now. I don't know how to act around them. What am I supposed to say?

The priest leads us through mass. We stand, sing, sit, and kneel. He's getting to the part right before Communion when we ask God to forgive us for all of our sins. The people in the choir stand up to take the Eucharist, but Mr. Butler just takes a blessing. I guess God hasn't forgiven his sins. I watch the rest of the parish file forward. Joe and Becky take the Eucharist, but Sue Butler doesn't.

After church Mom talks with Sue Butler and Mitch asks if Joe can come over to play. That afternoon Joe and Chad Davidson ride their bikes to our house. The four of us race dirt bikes through the field. Joe rides the fastest and we all take turns going off jumps.

Joe and I are in the same class at school, but I haven't seen him smile in a long time. When we finish racing Joe and Chad go home and even though Joe seems sad, I think he had fun. Maybe for a little bit he forgot about how things are at his house.

I go up to my room and look out my bedroom window at the tall pine trees swaying against the blue sky. If Mom or Dad got a divorce I wonder who I'd choose, Mom or Dad. I stare at the ceiling and even though I'm sad for Joe and Becky, I'm glad it's not my parents splitting up. I make the sign of the cross and pray that my parents won't ever separate. I pray for Mom and Dad like I haven't in a very long time.

DRINKING

Alcoholism runs in Mom's family. She says Grandma and Grandpa drink too much and when you do that, you don't make good decisions. Mom gets nervous when people drink and anytime someone drinks I wait for something bad to happen. Mom has us trained so whenever she asks, "What's the first thing to go when you're drinking?" we know to answer, "Your judgment."

When Chet's in the eleventh grade, he misses his 10:30 curfew. Bad judgment. I'm in bed asleep when he does get home but the next morning I can tell something is wrong.

Dad wants to tell Chet's baseball coach he was drinking so he gets kicked off the team. Chet signed a sports contract where he promised not to drink. Chet broke that, so Dad doesn't think he should play anymore. I can't believe they'd take baseball away from Chet. When Dad is mad, he's way meaner than Mom.

Mom convinces Dad not to tell the coach but they make it clear to Chet, and to the rest of us, if we drink, we will suffer the consequences.

MATT ROSE

At lunch I play dodge ball with the boys. Matt Rose and Daniel Callahan are on my team against Joe Butler, Cougar Caverhill, and Richard Eigeren. I'm pretty sure we can win. After we do, Matt calls Daniel and me over and he gives each of us a bag of Skittles.

"Thanks, Matt," I tell him. "Where'd you get all this candy?"

"I stopped at the store on the way to school."

At the start of recess the next day, Matt tells Daniel and me to come with him. We run across the playground, out the gate and across the street to a convenience store. I watch Matt and I'm pretty sure I see him put candy in his pocket, but then he goes to the counter and buys several bags of Skittles. When he offers me one, I take it, even though I know I shouldn't. I eat it before we get back to school. The bell rings for recess to end and no one notices we were gone.

Mrs. O'Rourke assigns a research project. We have to pick a topic and make a presentation. I decide to write about the women's suffrage movement. I can hardly believe that in this century they didn't let women vote.

I check out a book from the library and make a timeline to show during my presentation. I know exactly how Susan B. Anthony and Elizabeth Cady Stanton felt. I hate having boys say I can't do something just because I'm a girl.

On my day to present I walk to the front of the room with my timeline ready to show my classmates how far women have come. I start to read my report and my voice shakes. About halfway through, Matt starts laughing in the back of the room. My face is already red from nerves, but it turns even hotter. My hands are covered in sweat and the tears start. Don't cry. Only wimpy little girls cry. But the tears are about to come so I drop my poster and run out of the classroom. I sprint down the hall to the girls' bathroom and lean on the sink. I press down on the bar with my foot and water streams into my cupped hands. I rinse my face and look up into the mirror. I hate Matt Rose. I hate him, I hate him, I hate him.

When I go back to the classroom I've already decided. I am not forgetting this time. Matt will be nice to me, give me candy and pretend to be my friend. He'll try to make me forget about this like I forgot about the flag touching the ground and but I will not forget this time. Matt Rose is not my friend.

BETHY HURLEY

We pray for Bethy at school and I pray for her before I fall asleep at night. Sometimes she comes to school and I think my prayers are working, but that winter Bethy only shows up for school a couple of days. I still haven't figured out how to fold paper cranes. One spring morning—instead of praying for Bethy—we pray for her family because Bethy is gone. I cry when I hear about it. It doesn't seem fair.

Mrs. Hurley asks Mom if I will sing at Bethy's service. I'm glad I can do something to help. The church seems darker than usual on the day of the funeral because it's a sunny June day outside. Bethy's casket is open in the middle of the aisle. Mom says this is my chance to say goodbye just like she did at Greg Bob's funeral. I walk down the side aisle, far from the casket, to where the choir stands. Out of the corner of my eye, I see Bethy's family come in. I can't look at her mom and sisters because I know I'll cry and it's impossible to cry and sing at the same time. We sing "Hail Mary" and "Peace is Flowing like a River" and I try not to think about Bethy's little body in the middle of the church.

After singing "Beautiful" I go to sit with my family and Mrs. Hurley catches my eye and smiles. I can hardly believe she's not crying, that she can still smile, even now. I walk over, give her a hug and tell her I'm sorry.

I sit next to Mom until it's time for us to say goodbye to Bethy. I walk by her casket. The front half is propped open so we can see her face. I walk slowly, looking at the curved tips of my white shoes on the dark, red carpet until I'm standing in front of the casket. I look inside and see Bethy, but it's not really her. She hasn't looked like her for a long time. I wave goodbye, and walk quickly out of the church to wait at the car.

We don't talk about Bethy's funeral and it's quiet at our house. The sinking silence that comes with death pours over us, thick like syrup. I go to bed that night and try not to think about Bethy buried in the cemetery by Bear Creek and how dark it must be inside that coffin. I try not to think about Mr. and Mrs. Hurley or her sisters. What would I do if Chet, Laura or Mitch died? I stare into the darkness of my room and wonder what it feels like to be that close to death. Chet knows. He was there when Greg Bob died. Did he see his friend's soul leave his body? I fall asleep wondering.

During that last week of school Chet finishes up his baseball season and Laura runs track. On field day I win the hula-hoop contest and Mitch wins the ball toss. As summer starts everyone is so busy that no one notices the crusty residue of death sticking around the edges of the house on Jones Road.

CAMP

I've been waiting to go to Camp Cleawox ever since Laura went when I was little, back when we shared a room in the house on Shepard Road. The night before she left I watched her check items off a list as she packed. I climbed into my trundle bed and Laura turned off the light. The moon glowed off our Holly Hobby curtains and we sang songs from her camp songbook late into the night. That's the only reason I joined Girl Scouts in the first place, so that I could go to Girl Scout Camp some day.

I wake to the buzzer of my clock in the dark of 5:00 am. My heart pounds as soon as I remember, Camp Cleawox, and I smile. I rush through a shower and into the clothes I set out just like Laura did so many years ago. Downstairs, Mom and Dad are already up. Without a word, Dad grabs my bags and loads them in the car. The kitchen smells like cinnamon and Mom stands over the griddle, spatula in hand, staring at the sun rising over the Ochocos. I sprinkle Mom's perfect French toast with powdered sugar but I can't eat more than a couple of bites with all the butterflies in my stomach.

"Let's go, Nori," Dad yells from the garage.

"Have fun, honey. We'll see you on Friday." Mom looks tired as she hugs me goodbye. I run around the corner and skip steps to the garage.

I slam the car door and Dad backs the station wagon up the driveway. I wave at Mom standing in her robe until she disappears behind us.

Dawn light shimmers off the snow-capped mountains as we drive west. The car smells like Dad, soap and lotion. It's quiet until Dad starts his road trip quiz.

"So, Noriko, can you name all the mountains?"

"Bachelor is there," I respond with confidence. "Then Broken Top, and the Three Sisters. Then there's Three Fingered Jack, and Jefferson, or is it Washington?"

"Jefferson." Dad assures me and then come the trees: ponderosa pines, Douglas firs, junipers, Nobles, and dogwoods. I can point out each of them for the rest of this trip but on the next one Dad will have to teach me all over again.

"Tell me that camp story, Dad, the one with the watermelons."

Sun streams through the windshield, and Dad squints, thinking back to when he went to camp.

"Well, at camp, there was a watermelon patch and at night it got real cold, you know, so the watermelons got good and chilled. One night, me and my buddies snuck out. We crawled most of the way, to be sure we wouldn't get caught, and squeezed through a hole under the tall barbed wire fence to the watermelon patch. We took those huge watermelons and broke 'em open over our knees. We would stick our hands in and take out the hearts of the melons. The heart is the sweetest part and there are hardly any seeds in there, so we were just eating those hearts as fast as we could until we couldn't eat any more. I have never, never again in my whole life, tasted such delicious watermelon." Dad laughs and a smile stretches across his face.

Then it's quiet and Dad doesn't say anything. I sink into my seat and the seatbelt digs into my neck. I look at Dad's serious face and think of the books about camp that fill the bottom shelf of our bookcase. There are black and white photographs of little girls and whole families, numbered with tags and sitting on suitcases. Then there are wooden barracks and dusty streets, barbed wire fences and guard towers. My camp will be nothing like that and I feel like I should tell Dad that I know the difference, but I don't say anything. It's silent for the rest of the drive, just the empty mountain road and the rising sun.

We reach the drop off spot in Eugene where a big yellow bus waits. I suddenly don't want to go. Dad hands me my bags and hugs me. "Have fun. We'll miss you."

I load my bags under the bus and then climb the big steps. The smell of Dad and home are gone, replaced by bleach and plastic. I slide the length of an empty seat and peer past the smeary glass.

Dad stands at the car. I wave as the bus pulls away, and Dad smiles. He smiles at me as if he's thinking about the hearts of watermelons.

I fall asleep on the bus ride and when we get there we carry our bags down to our campsite. It's a warm day, but it stays cool in the shade of the trees. The Adirondack at our camp has eight bunks and Roo, our counselor, leads us to the lodge for lunch. I sit with my group on the front steps and watch the other campers. They don't look like the Girl Scout brochure. The brochure had pictures of white girls, Asian girls, Black girls and Latina girls, but just like my troop in Bend, I'm the only Girl Scout who isn't white. Faith and Loretta from my troop walk by. I wave but they must not see me because they just keep walking.

At camp we make s'mores and sing the same songs Laura taught me in our bedroom on Shepard Road. We hike across sand dunes to the beach and I win the hula contest. There is no barbed wire, no guard towers and no sneaking out to a watermelon patch. Instead there are trails, campfires, my cozy bunk and a freedom I've never felt before.

On the last day of camp, I'm ready to go home. Camp was fun but now that it's over I'm done being a Girl Scout.

GRASS CLIPPINGS

When I get home from Camp Cleawox, Chet is away at Young Life Camp and Laura is at basketball camp so Mitch and I have to do all the chores.

The house on Jones Road has grass that goes on forever. There's the front lawn, the huge backyard, and the parts by the ditch. It takes hours to mow all that grass. Our neighbors, the Cranks, have a riding mower and their lawn is half the size of ours.

Dad shows Mitch and I how to start the engine on our push mower. We have to wear shoes because Dad says, "If you wear sandals, you're just asking for a toe to get cut off." He fills the tank with gas. "Push the throttle to start, put your foot right here and pull this string up."

Mitch and I watch Dad start up the mower and then kill the engine. He wants both of us to try. Mitch goes first. He gets it started on the third try. The air fills with gas fumes and Dad kills the engine again. Now it's my turn. I step on the mower, grab the starter and pull the cord. Instead of roaring to life, the engine whines.

"You've got to pull it hard and fast," Dad instructs.

I lean over and try again. "I'm not tall enough," I tell Dad but he insists I can do it.

I try three more times and now I'm tired. I step off the mower and Mitch reminds me that if he can do it, I should be able to.

I wait to catch my breath and then try one more time. I yank as hard as I can and the motor catches. It spins and little rocks kick up from the asphalt, stinging my legs.

Later that week Dad tells me it's my turn to mow the lawn. I wear jean shorts, a white tank top and my oldest pair of tennis shoes. At least I can get a tan while I'm mowing the lawn.

I push the mower to the end of the backyard. I love the smell of gasoline and the satisfaction of starting the engine. But after a few trips up and down the long backyard, my arms ache and the sun pounds the top of my head. I think about all of the times Chet and Laura have walked up and down the yard like I am now, snipping away each grass blade's tip. My eyes water and I sneeze every other minute from allergies. I count my steps to make it go faster, and finally toss the last bag of clippings into the compost where they will eventually turn brown for Dad to scatter over the garden in the fall.

The soles of my shoes are green and my clothes are sweaty all the way through. I roll the lawn mower into the garage and head in to the kitchen where I drink three full glasses of water. In the bathroom, I strip off sweaty clothes, and step into the shower. The tan-line fades as I scrub off the dirt and sweat. The smell of gasoline, grass and grime washes down the drain.

I relax in the family room but even with the TV on, it's too quiet. With Chet and Laura gone, the house feels empty. I'm bored so I grab the last purple Popsicle from the freezer and walk outside, atop freshly clipped grass, to the footbridge. My toes dangle in the water and as I finish my Popsicle, I think about Bethy Hurley and what her sisters might be doing this summer. I hope they're staying busy, taking tennis lessons and going to the pool. In the silence of grass growing around me, I imagine it's even quieter at their house than it is at ours.

SINKING AGAIN

It's hot the day Chet comes home from Young Life camp. He drops his bags on the floor with a thud and smiles, but the smile is forced, like he's a puppet and someone's pulling strings attached to his face. I give him a hug, because I missed him and I want to feel him, to know it's him even though he looks different. Laura, Mitch and I gather around our brother in the kitchen.

"What happened to you at that camp," Laura asks with a sneer. "Did they brainwash you?"

"No," Chet says as he opens up the freezer. "Who ate all of the grape Popsicles?"

I twist the yellow phone cord around my finger forcing all of the blood into my red fingertip.

"So, what was it like?" Laura prods. "Did you sit around praying all day?"

Chet drinks down a glass of milk and then talks fast. "No. We went water skiing and swimming everyday. We did this zip-line-thing where you fly over the tops of the trees and then drop into the water. But it was the people. The most amazing people were there. Really, you have to go." Chet's eyes skip over each of us. "It will change your life. Seriously." He pours another glass of milk, drinks it and then says he's tired. He goes upstairs to take a nap.

I sit in my room upstairs with the window open, trying to stay cool. I think about the zip line Chet described and imagine him suspended from a wire, gliding across a blue lake. The water glistens in the summer sun and my brother's real smile shines from his tan face instead of this fake, too-big smile he wears today.

Loud music comes from Chet's room so there's no way he's taking a nap. The lyrics "Sunday, Bloody Sunday" come through loud and clear even though his door is shut tight.

I'm hot even though I'm imagining that cool lake up at Young Life camp. I wonder if there's something else wrong with Chet, aside from him forgetting how to smile. He doesn't usually hang out in his room. In the summer Chet goes to baseball practice or plays wiffle ball in the backyard.

I go downstairs and find Mom in the kitchen making potato salad. The kitchen is hot and filled with steam from the pot boiling on the stove. Mom peels the shells off hard-boiled eggs at the sink. I climb up a stool at the breakfast bar and watch her. "Mom, do you know what Chet's doing?"

"I think Ron Lowe is coming over in a little bit. He's tired from camp so don't bother him."

"Is he okay?" I ask. "He's acting kind of weird."

Mom looks at me as if she just realized I was there. "What do you mean, weird?"

I shrug, unable to explain the changes I've noticed in Chet, the way he's talking so fast; how his smile has shifted.

Mom looks back at the egg in her hand. "He's probably just tired. You remember how you felt when you came back from camp. I'm sure he's fine. Don't worry."

I walk back upstairs unconvinced. Chet isn't telling us something and I need to find out what's really going on.

The doorbell rings and Chet flings his bedroom door open. "I got it," he yells as he sprints from his room and down the stairs. I grab the portable tape recorder, tiptoe across the hall and push the door open. Mitch and Chet's room is always messy, clothes everywhere and it smells like dirty underwear and sweat. I listen for footsteps coming back up stairs but there's nothing yet. I open the closet door, set the tape recorder behind a pair of basketball shoes, press record and retreat back to my room.

Chet and his friend hang out in his room for a while and after they leave I retrieve the tape recorder. It's tough to hear them but what I can hear doesn't sound very important. I try to trust Mom. Maybe there isn't anything wrong with Chet after all.

Three days later, Mom and Dad take Chet to the hospital. I hear the garage door open when they come home late that night and Chet's not with them. Laura and I head down stairs to find out what's going on.

"Where is he? Can we go see him?" Laura asks.

Mom and Dad look at one another and Dad shakes his head. "It's not that kind of sick."

"He'll be okay, girls," Mom tells us. "We're doing everything we can to help your brother."

Again, they tell us not to worry.

On Sunday afternoon, Mom and Dad call a family meeting. We sit at the breakfast room table and stare at Chet's empty chair.

"Now, you know Chet is in the hospital." Dad starts the meeting like that, no checking in or anything. "He's having a hard time right now. He isn't sleeping and he's very angry about being in the hospital. He has to stay there until we figure out what's wrong with him. If any of you have a hard time sleeping or if you hear voices, you have to tell us. Understand? Do you have any questions?"

I have a million questions. What's going on with Chet? Why does he need to be in the hospital? Where are the voices coming from? Is it contagious? What are they doing to him in the hospital? What happens to someone if they don't sleep? But Mom and Dad don't look like they want to answer any of my questions so I just sit there. I recognize this feeling. It's exact same way I felt when we picked Mitch up at the airport. He didn't want to come with us and we made him.

"When's he coming home?" Mitch's voice cracks when he asks.

"We don't know, but hopefully in another day or two."

I stare at the yellow wallpaper in the breakfast room that suddenly looks faded and dusty. We sit in the quiet until Mom says, "That's all we wanted to tell you."

The family meeting is over and Laura, Mitch and I go up to our bedrooms and hide behind closed doors.

Chet comes home a few days later but he doesn't seem like Chet. He's quiet and distant and goes straight to his room. I wonder if he talks to Mitch late at night but I never hear anything.

Chet starts going to counseling. I wonder if he's crazy but Mom and Dad both start counseling too and we can't all be crazy. Chet sees Dr. Gibson and after a while he starts to seem more like himself. He doesn't really seem happy though. When he smiles it's like he has to tell his face what to do. He can't seem to smile out of nowhere and I wonder if he'll ever be happy again.

MIDDLE SCHOOL

Summer ends and Chet starts his senior year. He's busy with football practice and Laura has volleyball daily doubles. Mitch is in seventh grade at Pilot Butte Junior High and for the first time in my life I'm the only Nakada at St. Francis.

In the rush of school starting, I forget about the strange silence lingering around our house, about the summer when Chet couldn't sleep, heard voices, and ended up in the hospital.

On the first day of school Loretta and Faith don't talk to me and I can tell it's going to be a bad year. So, when Mom picks me up that afternoon and asks if I want to go to Pilot Butte Junior High for the sixth grade I say, "Sure, why not?" I don't want to stay at St. Francis if I don't have any friends. Besides, all through elementary I felt like I was missing out on something. The only kids I knew were the same ones I went to school with for six years. At Pilot Butte I'll get to meet new kids. I'll finally be the new kid and I'll get a fresh start.

After Mom fills out the paperwork in the office at Pilot Butte a student walks me up the steep pathway to the sixth grade building. The whole campus smells like juniper and it's so much bigger than St. Francis. I look around at the buildings and wonder what's going on inside those classrooms. Mitch is somewhere in the seventh grade hall but this is his first year here too, so he won't be much help.

Mrs. Gregory's room is small and after she signs a paper she points to a desk. Joe Butler sits two desks behind me and it's nice having someone familiar there even though Joe is quiet, especially since the divorce.

Mrs. Gregory hands me math and reading tests to see how I compare with the other kids. Every so often, I look around and try to guess who might be my new friend.

At recess—which isn't called recess in middle school, it's called break—I walk out to the field. A bunch of boys play catch with a football and I wonder what girls do during break. The boys aim the football through a board with a hole in it. Mike Bjorvick, from my baseball team two summers ago, winds up and tosses. He misses and the ball rolls toward me. I grab the ball, line my fingers up on the laces, and throw. Maybe it's luck, but the ball spirals right through the hole. The boys' mouths fall open, shocked, and as the bell rings they walk toward me. A tall, dark-haired boy asks my name and teases the boys who missed because Nori could make it and they couldn't. It's strange hearing this boy I've never met before say my name. I walk away from the football field with a few girls from my class and glance back over my shoulder at the boys arguing about their football prowess.

The next day, Mrs. Gregory tells me to stay in her room for math. Some kids leave and other students come in. I move up to the front row and Robert, the dark-haired boy from break yesterday, sits next to me. He's tall and skinny. He has olive skin like mine and I wonder if he might be Asian too.

I spend the rest of the week trying to figure out how Pilot Butte is different from St. Francis. First, it's much bigger (St. Francis only had one sixth grade class and Pilot Butte has six). The cool kids are in Mrs. Drew and Mrs. Hawkins room. They have two teachers, one for the morning and one for the afternoon. Gabe Sheerer is in that class. Gabe looks like he could be in the eighth grade and there are seventh grade girls who like him. I'm not in a very good class. No one ever says, "Oh, you're lucky," when I tell them I'm in Mrs. Gregory's class. Even though math was never my favorite subject, I like it when other kids who are smart at math come in, and I like sitting with Robert. He's half Polynesian and it's the first time I have a class with someone else who's Asian.

Robin Crank, my neighbor across the street, is in the cool class. As kids, Robin and I occasionally played together. We sold lemonade on the side of the road and made almost ten dollars. Robin had a Fresh 'N Fancy make-up kit. She gave me a makeover one summer afternoon but when I got home Laura made fun of me.

Apparently, Laura and I aren't the kind of girls who wear make-up. Robin had a tetherball court in her backyard but St. Francis didn't have tetherball so she always beat me.

Once I start going to Pilot Butte, Robin and I walk to school together. We head down Revere to Bianca Weston's house. Both the Cranks and the Westons are a lot richer than us. Bianca and Robin wear Esprit shirts, Guess jeans and Swatch watches. The Weston's house is huge and spotless. Mrs. Weston answers the door in her bathrobe and yells upstairs for Bianca to hurry. Robin and I stand in the entry hall, waiting. Mrs. Weston says she likes Robin's outfit and one day she says I have pretty hands.

When Bianca is ready, we walk slowly toward school and talk about the cutest boys, which girls are cool, and who's stuck up. Robin and Bianca are nice on the walk, but once we get to school, we go our separate ways. At lunch they sit at a table with all the cute boys like Gabe Sheerer and Ezra Ross.

At dinner one night I tell Mom about my walk to school and Laura asks if I'm really friends with Bianca Weston. "Yeah, I guess," I say.

"Yeah, she is," Mitch says and he rolls his eyes. He hates all of my new friends.

"That's crazy," Chet says with a scowl. "Her dad used to yell at us for cutting through their yard and now you walk right up to their front door."

I've heard this story before, but didn't know it was Bianca's dad. When we lived in the house on Shepard Road, a shortcut ran next to the irrigation ditch and through the Weston's front yard. Chet and Ray Garretson were taking the shortcut when Mr. Weston told them to walk around, that his yard was not a sidewalk. Chet and Ray ran down the shortcut anyway and left Mr. Weston yelling at an empty dirt path. The next day, Chet told Laura they were still going to use the path. "I'm not scared of that guy." But when they reached the Weston's house, Mr. Weston was sitting on their long front porch with a shotgun across his knees. They never used the shortcut again.

"I can't believe you're friends with Bianca Weston," Laura says.

I shrug. What do Chet, Laura or Mitch know about my friends? What do Chet, Laura and Mitch know about me?

CHET'S RETURN

I get so caught up in my life at Pilot Butte that I forget to worry about Chet, but when Mom, Dad, Laura, Mitch and I pile into the station wagon and head to Portland to watch Chet's playoff football game, I remember.

It's cold for November and the road over the Cascades is slick with black ice. Mom closes her eyes most of the trip but she's even more concerned about Chet riding the team bus on this icy mountain pass.

The drive usually takes three hours, but today it takes almost five. We finally arrive in Portland just before the game starts. Half of the field is frozen and covered in ice. I scan the stadium for Chet. He plays cornerback and special teams so when the Cougars are on defense or when there's a kick off or punt we all stand up and cheer for number 42.

The players on both teams struggle for traction on the frozen field and neither team scores. In the final quarter it's fourth and long for Gresham so they set up to punt.

I spot Chet's number 42 waiting on the right side of the backfield, almost in the other team's end zone. The Gresham center hikes and the punter sends the ball flying through the air, right to my big brother.

Chet catches the ball and sprints toward the sideline.

He gets a block and shakes off a tackle. He runs up the sideline so all that's in front of him is a field of solid ice.

I scream. We all scream, the whole family, the whole crowd. We jump and cheer, hoping Chet won't slip, that he'll make it to the end zone.

I watch my brother. I watch him run like I've watched him my whole life. I've watched him run through snow in the backyard, down a basketball court, and from first to third on a base hit to the right side. He's always been so big to me, but out on that field, with all those other football players, he looks tiny.

Chet runs fast, but as he sprints down that football field, it looks like he's moving in slow motion.

20 yards, 15, 10, 5...

Chet skates on top of the ice for the last five yards and glides into the end zone. He jumps into the air and his teammates tackle him in celebration. We cheer and as the score changes Chet jogs to the sideline.

With Mountain View in the lead, we wait for the final minutes to wind down. The last seconds tick off the clock and the crowd's roar cuts through the frozen air.

The team celebrates on the field and Chet takes off his helmet. His coaches and teammates slap him on the back and mess up his dark hair. Chet looks up into the stands, searching for us. We wave and yell his name until finally he spots us and waves back.

I can't stop staring because he's smiling. Under the bright lights of the icy stadium my brother's face glows. Chet is really smiling again.

LAST CHRISTMAS

The first snow of the winter falls earlier than usual and I get to ski the entire mountain with the cousins. The Nakadas say this is their last holiday trip to Bend and I wonder how Christmas will feel without a house full of cousins teasing me and aunties and uncles telling stories around the table. I'm counting the months we have left as a family too. Next fall, Chet will go away to college and we'll hardly ever be together as a family anymore.

We decorate our tree with Auntie Grace's ceramic stars and bells and Auntie Jo's crocheted snowflakes. We head up to the mountain to ski all week and on Christmas Eve we go out to Eddie's Canton for Chinese.

After dinner we light the last of the advent candles and Mom reads *The Night Before Christmas* even though we haven't believed in Santa for years. Before bed, our cousin Mike snaps a picture. The flash captures all of us dressed up in our Christmas Eve best.

Mom pulls out an old album from that first Christmas when all the Nakadas went to a photographer in the Wagner Mall. I imagine the people of Bend staring as forty Asians walked through the mall and into that photo studio.

I study the faces in that fading photograph. All of Dad's brothers, sisters, in-laws and kids were strangers to me then, but now I know them all. Back then my uncles weren't grey and several of my cousins were the same age I am now. I was only three then and I smiled from my seat on the floor. Everyone wore plaid shirts with wide-collars, bell-bottom jeans, and long bangs hung over dark eyes. Laura, Chet and I pepper this Nakada family portrait, different from everyone, belonging to everyone and to no one.

I gaze into this picture from before Mitch came.
Before Greg Bob died.
Before *The King and I*.
Before I started school.

Before we moved to the house on Jones Road.
Before Mom and Dad started fighting.
Before Mom got sick.
Before Goldie and Neko, Tiger and Bob the Cat.
Before Bethy died.
Before Chet's smile faded and returned.
Before this last Christmas.

I study this sea of family faces receding into the distance and fear I'll wash away.

MOCHI TSUKI

Mom and Dad decide we'll drive to Los Angeles for the New Year since family vacations will soon be a thing of the past. We load into the station wagon and pack our bags with shorts and t-shirts we haven't worn since August.

This will be our first chance to see the Japanese tradition of *mochi* pounding. Even though there are machines for making *mochi*, the Nakadas meet at Uncle Yosh's house in Baldwin Hills every New Year to make it by hand. I've never seen or tasted *mochi*. To me, Mochi is a dog from a distant memory.

On the first day of the trip we drive to Davis and stay with Uncle Yoshio and Auntie Kimi. Uncle Yoshio has a train set. Mitch and I watch the train pass through a miniature world. In the other room, Auntie Kimi shows Laura how to play the xylophone.

The next day we drive all day and arrive in the brilliant sunlight of Uncle Yosh and Auntie Suma's house. They have a little white dog named Sukoshi that I follow into the backyard where I can see the Hollywood sign through a misty haze.

Aunties and Uncles rush around getting things ready for *mochi tsuki*. A huge carved out stone sits in the center of the yard like an enormous mortar. Two buckets of water hold heavy wooden mallets and I have to use both hands to pick one up.

Uncle Yosh carries a tray of steaming rice from a camping stove and dumps it inside the carved out stone. Two of my uncles use wooden mallets to mash the rice until in comes together in one giant glob. Then they are ready to pound and it takes three people. Two men alternate hitting the rice. A third person, with a quick hand, flips and slaps the rice between each smack to keep it from sticking. They pound, turn, pound, turn until sweat glistens from foreheads and flexed arms.

When the rice becomes a creamy, goopy glob, the turner scrapes it from the stone and places it on a table covered with rice flour. My aunties and cousins show me how to separate the *mochi* into bite-sized pieces and wrap it around a ball of *an*. I've never seen *an* before but it looks like chocolate. Auntie Grace tells me it's made from crushed sweet beans.

Once a batch is done, the process begins again and a rhythm develops: pounding, turning, cutting and wrapping. Blisters and rice flour cover hands. We pound forever and by the time the sun sets, men's shoulders ache and women's fingers crack and peel.

The plain *mochi*, a smooth white disk without *an*, sits soft and warm in my hand. I take a big bite and the *mochi* churns in my mouth like a huge glob of tasteless bubble gum. I chew and chew, but it doesn't break down. When I finally swallow the dense mass it sticks in my throat like a too-big potato. Then I try a piece with the chocolate colored *an* inside. It tastes nothing like chocolate and the chunks of sweet bean penetrate the gooey rice. I curb the gag reflex climbing up my throat and swallow the chunks whole.

Two days of *mochi tsuki*, sushi, and warm weather end and we start the long drive back to Oregon. I stare out the car windows already missing the comfort of family I feel around the Nakadas. The lights of a million lives flash by at 65 miles per hour. I wish I could slow down; peek into the homes pulsing in the night. I imagine a little girl like me, playing with a puppy even though she's too young to remember it. Somewhere out there, a family strives to hold on to traditions like we do making *mochi*. Maybe they name their orange cat Naranjo, or their little dog Perrito, like we did with Neko, and Mochi.

As the lights fade to a distant glow, I look back toward the city and imagine, somewhere in all of those lives, a little girl who is a lot like me. Maybe she rides in a car thinking about someone living far away from these lights and people. Even though our lives are separated by so much I wonder if she imagines the world through eyes like mine.

THE VIEW FROM HERE

I sit cross-legged on my bed looking out the window. The sill was painted shut years ago so I have to push with all of my weight to get it open. I lean out until my nose grazes the screen. Thousands of stars fill the sky and the moon is half-full, sending light shimmering across the asphalt and the dewy grass. Early spring air filters through the dusty screen.

The view outside my window hasn't changed much over the past few years. Still, every night, I look for something different, a constellation in a different spot in the sky, or a light turning on in a neighbor's house. Sometimes I just close my eyes and listen to a chorus of crickets singing into the night.

The trees are bigger than when we first moved to this house. I've watched them change every year, with every season. In winter their branches sag under heavy snow. It's spring when they turn white and pink with flowers. All summer the view outside is green until the trees turn gold and red. The leaves fall and the branches are left bare again.

I know what to expect from the trees outside my window, but what happens inside our house is always different. Chet will leave for college in a few months and in two years Laura will go too. Then it will be Mitch's turn and then mine.

Bits of me fall like leaves and drift downstream. I wish I could pull them in before they catch in the current and float away.

I talk with my friends from school more than my family now. Everyone is busy, constantly coming and going from the house on Jones Road.

I look into the star-filled sky, at the Big Dipper hanging above the horizon.

I've never been able to picture a future beyond these forests, mountains, rivers and lakes. Does that mean I'll die young?

I can't imagine my prince charming, so maybe I'll never get married, or maybe I'll end up somewhere so far away, so different from Bend, that I can't picture it at all.

From my bedroom window, gazing up into a starlit sky, I wish I could skip ahead, fast-forward through time and know who I will be in ten, twenty, fifty years. I want to know where Chet, Laura and Mitch will be. Where will Mom and Dad end up?

I look up into the arms of the trees growing around me and miss all the yesterdays, but I feel even more anxious for tomorrow and every day to come.

A cool breeze blows down from the mountain. I pull my head in from the window, lie back on my pillow and breathe. I stretch the sheets and blankets tight around me. I close my eyes and wait for sleep while the crickets sing into the night.

unending gratitude to...
   my family for helping me tell this version of our history.
   the Nakada and Barry families.
   the small town of Bend, which doesn't exist anymore, but still holds in its forests, mountains, rivers and streets the memories of my childhood.
   the St. Francis School and Parish (before it was a McMinnemans).
   the Antioch MFA program in Los Angeles, all of my mentors and fellow writers.
   David Gantt, for your constant support.

Made in the USA
Lexington, KY
16 December 2010